Where's My Rosary?

WHERE'S MY ROSARY?

JANE MAWER

GWASG PANTYCELYN

© Jane Mawer 2003

Gwasg Pantycelyn

ISBN 1-903314-53-4

Published with the support of the
Welsh Books Council

Thanks to Saint Joseph's Church, Pwllheli,
and Father Harry Clarke; to the Mary Strand Trust helping the
sick, the poor and the elderly
and Joseph Kelly, editor of *The Universe*, for their support.

This book was translated into Welsh by Alwena Williams
Cover: Welsh Books Council

Printed in Wales
by Gwasg Pantycelyn, Caernarfon

CONTENTS

INTRODUCTION

Jane Mawer is an eagle with broken wings. Crippled by rheumatoid arthritis and unable to leave the nest of her wheelchair, she is still a free spirit who is able to fly where only the bravest eagles dare. Told in an extraordinarily simple and honest way, this book is a gripping story of the power of the human spirit to rise above the most daunting physical handicaps. It will make you realise the pain and frustration of those who suffer from rheumatoid arthritis.

At the age of eighteen she had her first hip replacement which had to be renewed some years later. She refused to be a victim of her disability and as far as possible lived a normal life. There were times of despair in her life which tempted her to throw in the towel and surrender. A typical example was the death of her first baby when she was a young mother:

> My baby Josephine Mary died aged one. It was January 31st, 1987. The date is branded on my heart. At twenty to one on a normal Saturday afternoon, *Grandstand* on the telly, my interest-free microwave needed paying and my life was over. Her birth had been uneventful, considering I had an artificial hip and knee.

Jane's life was not over. It was only just beginning.

The style of the book is most unusual – short sentences which are neither spin-offs nor platitudes but which unleash truths quarried from the pit of deep physical pain.

Each chapter has a story to tell of how Jane progressed in her understanding of suffering to which she committed herself in trust to God whom she loved as her father. In times of personal tragedy she spoke to him in straightforward, honest language. She is angry with God, but never bitter, or cynical. This is a deeply spiritual book which will help the reader to reflect on what life and faith are all about. You will return to it time and again and always its deep insights will give you pause for thought. It is no ordinary autobiography. It is the story of the eagle who flew very high without ever leaving her wheelchair. I recommend it completely as an inspiring book which is needed in our troubled times.

Mgr. Michael Buckley, D.D.

PREFACE

"A dark vicious enemy that's made its home in me." If home is anything, then it is the place where one is real. It is the place where one moves out into the world, and the place where things ultimately make sense.

This book is about home.

But here, home is not simply the significant location where people dwell and are rooted, it is also the body, a specific body, which pain inhabits and feels at ease in.

Jane's body is pain's home.

Like God, pain did not have to be invited in. Like God, pain was just there. The three of them, a human and divine trinity; God, Pain, Jane, living together in passionate intimacy.

This book is full of domestic detail and the rawness that is the stuff of family relationships. And God is in that family, and so is pain. Often it is difficult to pull God and pain apart, the edges are blurred, the boundaries fuzzy, just like family. At one point she says, "paradoxically it hurts more with God because the sense of abandonment feels worse". That is the essence of the whole book, an essence that makes it startlingly different from most "spiritual" tracts. Jane "hurts", she "feels", she "weeps". But she also "complains", "swears", and is angry and full of fear.

Her body won't do what it is told. It can't hold things or hurry about. She is aware of the startling differences between herself and others, and all the assumptions that "healthy" people make, and all they take for granted.

God won't go away, neither will pain, neither will death. One after the other, daughter, mother, father, best friend, grandmother all die, and her grieving congeals into one open wound of sorrow.

This is her gospel of pain. Her domestic dialogue with God. You won't find here a rarefied spirituality, but you will be witness to God as inside a real house in which real people eat and do the washing up. In which there is all the domestic complexity of simply living alongside each other and of being next to each other.

Rev. Randolph Ellis

ACKNOWLEDGEMENTS

- To my mother and father, whose courage and endurance in the face of adversity has been their lasting gift and rich legacy that death cannot destroy.

- To Paul, my patient and loving husband of eighteen years, for being my "rock" when the world was a dark place.

- Thank God for my daughter Rebecca Anne, now fourteen, for giving me the reason to get up in the morning.

- To my brother, Lt. Col. Richard John Pierce, and my sisters Claire and Anne and their families for their unfailing love and support.

- To Maldwyn Thomas and June Jones and all at Gwasg Pantycelyn, and the staff of the Welsh Books Council for their belief in the ramblings of an ordinary mother with a tale that may be of value to others.

- Mrs Gwyneth Sol Owen, my English teacher, who recognised my passion for literature and rewarded my efforts in the only subject that fired my soul.

- To Helena Rogowska who typed the manuscript under great stress without complaint. She boosted my confidence and inspired me to keep writing when my reserves were low.

- My deepest gratitude to Randolph Ellis, friend and counsellor, for mending a broken and disillusioned heart. Without him, I would be alive but not living. He gave me the courage to be "me" and told me that it was okay to be human.

- Had it not been for Fr. Harry Clarke, our parish priest, I would not have read Thomas Merton, C. S. Lewis, Anthony De Mello and the great spiritual giants. His love of books and generosity of heart renewed my faith in a loving and personal Christ.

- Heartfelt thanks to Mgr. Michael Buckley, an eminent writer and healer who has helped thousands of people during his ministry. Readers of *The Universe* will be touched by his ability to make you feel as if you are the only person in the world, loved and cherished. A truly humble and holy man.

- My closest and dearest friends need no reference. They know who they are and how much I value their love and understanding.

- Thanks to Mr Joseph Kelly, editor of *The Universe,* for giving me a break all those years ago. I owe him a huge debt of gratitude for his belief in me as a gospel writer and for giving me the confidence to embark on a writing career.

- My thanks on behalf of his "children" to the late Dr D. J. Ward, an eminent Rheumatologist at Gobowen Hospital, and to Dr Bernard Morgan and his team at the Pain Clinic for their understanding and compassion in dealing with a chronic pain sufferer.

- I want to thank God for His mercy and love for a sinner like me. I thank Him for my blessings and graces and for staying awake when everyone else has gone to sleep.

Jane Mawer, Pwllheli, January 2003

DEDICATION

TO JOSEPHINE MARY
1986–1987
Ni chwsg cariad
(Love does not sleep)

Where's My Rosary? is dedicated to
the memory of my late grandmother,
PHILOMENA GRIFFITHS.
Her mother, Josephine Mary Roberts, came over from
Ireland many years ago and she was one of the founder
members of the Catholic Church in Pwllheli. Included in
the text is a prayer to St Philomena. I pay tribute to her
namesake to Josephine Mary, whose faith and
perseverance never wavered as she prayed the rosary in a
strange and foreign land. This book belongs to those
dearly departed who gave us the Catholic teaching and
dared us to be different.

"BUT SHE IS AN ANGEL IN HEAVEN"

My baby Josephine Mary died aged one. It was January 31st, 1987. The date is branded on my heart. At twenty to one on a normal Saturday afternoon, *Grandstand* on the telly, my interest-free microwave needed paying and my life was over. Her birth had been uneventful, considering I had an artificial hip and knee.

I loved Josie from the moment I set eyes on her. Spiky hair and blue eyes. We lived with my dad after my mother died. He was war-disabled, although now a white collar worker for the County Council.

He was a great support. Pushing the pram when Josie wouldn't settle. He had lost his right arm in Normandy but could manage a pram well. Josie took the sting out of his terrible loss. Ours was a close family. My mother was a Catholic and Dad a Baptist.

Paul, my husband, was in the Merchant Navy. He got married in his Officer's uniform. We were in love. How little we knew of what was to come.

Josie's cancer, a rare form of neuroblastoma, was diagnosed in September, 1986. Anne, my twin, was expecting Mark, now 13. Claire, my big sister, was working in Essex. It was approaching the first anniversary of my mother's death and we hoped that things would get better. Paul's father died suddenly in August and I took Josie down to Bristol. Dad paid for a taxi for us from Pwllheli to Bristol; he was that kind of a man.

Paul had to go back to sea. I missed him deeply but I had Dad for company and my gorgeous little girl.

Dad was retiring in September and on the date of his celebrations, Josie, Paul and I stayed home. Josie was ill. Dad wanted to cancel everything. I told him not to be daft. We were fine.

Paul left for Southampton. The following day was bedlam.

Dad was in the garden. He came in and said that Josie was breathing oddly. This was the war veteran who had been placed in a tent for the dying by mistake.

I called the doctor. She took one look at Josie and told us to get to Bangor Hospital immediately and she then literally ran out of our house. I thought that this was strange. I felt myself becoming numb as we arrived in Bangor. Meningitis was my biggest fear. Cancer is not something you associate with an eight month old baby.

We were told the devastating news a few hours later. We were to go to Alder Hey Children's Hospital the next day. I wanted to take Josie home. There were not very keen but, since Claire was a nurse and we seemed sensible enough, they agreed.

Dad gave me a whisky. Auntie Phil was cleaning and I felt as if a horse had kicked me in the stomach. How can you look at your baby – the same beautiful child – and fear that she may be dying?

There are no words to describe the pain. I was worried about Paul. I was convinced that the stress would give Dad a heart attack and I could barely bring myself to look at Josie.

I changed her nappy. There was this huge tumour in her stomach. It had come from nowhere. She was fine last week. She looked at me and I tickled her and kissed her and made her laugh. She laughed and fell asleep.

I needed my mum. Oh God, how were we going to cope? The family were wonderful.

Alder Hey confirmed our worst nightmare and I could see pitiful bald heads and ravaged faces around me. This is Hell, I thought. Parents looking permanently hung over. Exhausted. Terrified.

The day room was where we smoked and drank tea. That room saw more heartbreak than any other room in the world. Hopes were raised. Sarah's blood count is up. We were pleased. Donna's parents were devastated. The news for them was bad. We hurt with them. It is a peculiar kind of camaraderie. Ups and downs. We swore, drank tea, felt physically ill for each other.

Josie started her chemotherapy and I sat with her in a hard armchair while the poison was pumped into her system. I had to be strong for her. My arthritis went through the shock. I took my pills and forgot about myself. Josie needed her mother now and I could not, would not, let her down.

She perked up for a while and we came home. I was trying to keep things normal for her. She was fed liquidated roast dinners with apple sauce and yoghurts. I was feeding her better.

My real friends and family were brilliant. Help with practical things, like washing and tumble drying the clothes. My aunties, my mother's sisters, were stars.

Paul and I went out occasionally to block the pain. Dad would insist we needed a break. I ran out of the house, desperate for the drink that would anaesthetise my breaking heart. I feel guilty now. We only went out when we knew she was OK. I have often wondered since what it must have looked like to the outside world. Josie has cancer; how can they enjoy themselves? We were not enjoying ourselves. We were desperate. Drowning in fear and ugliness. The drink was a couple of hours' escape from 24-hour Hell. Anyhow, anyone who judged us was not capable of being human. I was twenty-four years old. I was witnessing, we were witnessing, horrors beyond knowing.

Josie lived for a further five months. A lot of our time was spent at Alder Hey. Anne, by now heavily pregnant, cooked for us and provided us with that home from home feeling. I slept on a makeshift bed by Josie's cot. We took it in turns.

I remember one night, she was crying and I sneaked her into my bed where we snuggled, breaking every hospital rule, and dozed off together. She had a portacath in her chest. Her bones stuck out like those poor African children Her spiky black hair fell out and she began to look like all the others in this God-forsaken Hellhole.

Couples argued over ridiculous things. I had been picking a fight and I ran off to a room we had at the hospital. I went on my knees and cried out to God, "take her if you want her, but please God, don't let her suffer".

I rarely broke down, but things were going wrong and I thought that if I told God what he wanted to hear, then he would let us keep her. A feeble, immature, but decidedly desperate, "Thy will be done".

My mother's words, "God is good," flooded my brain. I wanted to agree. How could I? My daughter was dying. Yes, mother, He's very good. I was afraid of God. He had decided that I should be ill from a young age. He had taken my mother away before we could say goodbye. And now this. Are we talking about the same God? I was afraid of my blasphemy. When I said, "take her if you want her" I did not really mean it, and there wasn't much talk of God in the day room.

He was there, though. Why? Because ordinary folk, the average mother and father who love their children, were becoming heroes.

We shared the tea bags and our cigarettes. The lads went out to buy cans at the end of a hellish day. No one knew what tomorrow would bring. There was a wonderful sense of love here.

I remember staring out of the window late at night after Josie had settled. The people of Liverpool were asleep, living ordinary lives, and here we were. In the bowels of the worst possible scenarios.

Ward rounds came and went. I hated it when they touched her – my baby. She's mine. Leave her alone. She cried as soon as she saw a white coat. I wanted to kill anyone who hurt her. And hurt her they had to do if she was to have any chance of living.

We had a good Christmas. What do you buy a child who is dying? Everything we could afford. A big Teddy Ruxpin, a teddy that spoke, a little drum kit, loads of balloons and more.

Dad had a bug on Christmas day and he and Josie, who had developed an extraordinary bond, shared their turkey sandwiches by the coal fire in our front room. Later, he often spoke of those precious memories. They were his alone and he hugged them close.

She celebrated her first birthday on January 25th. We had a big party for the family, the extended family and their children. When it was over, she began to fail. Next day at Alder Hey they told us that it was hopeless. The tumours were in her head, everywhere. This is it.

The Consultant, I can't remember his name, told us in the corridor. Paul said, "I could murder a pint". I glared at him and we went back to our baby.

My nerves were well and truly gone. I phoned Anne to tell Dad that treatment had stopped. I didn't have the courage to do that myself. What a horrible transference – she was expecting a baby any day. I couldn't tell Dad. I loved him too much. Josie was everything to him.

We came home and just in time. The GP refused to come out when we were unsure about the morphine dosage. Claire, Paul, John and I took turns to nurse her. I would not give her morphine. I thought that I would be killing her if I did. She needed morphine, my sweet baby; it's just that I couldn't do it.

I called the priest, Father Tony Jones, and he came over. She was given all the right prayers. A little rosary around her neck. I knew she was without sin but, even in my immature faith, I wanted her to have every blessing going.

Just before she died, I picked her up, out of her snug pushchair. She opened her eyes – a tear dropped onto my shoulder. She sighed and died in my arms. Paul and I were with her at the end of her struggle for life.

I carried her upstairs. Her cot was clean and waiting for her. Father said the prayers. He said he had never felt such a strong sense of God before in his life. This was a priest who had visited many holy places. Claire and my aunty laid her out in her nice new outfit. I wanted her to have a huge cot duvet over her, to keep her warm and snug.

I made a conscious decision to remember her nice and

warm. I still had images of my dead mother in my head. She was my mother but part of her was gone. Now I know that it was her soul.

I went downstairs and threw away all the baby reminders. I don't remember much. My auntie cooked us a lovely meal and I ate like a horse.

Visitors came and went. Richard, my brother, took Dad for a walk. Father Jones was kind. My cousins were tremendous but she was gone. It was all over. I was empty. Numb. Tired. Detached. Disassociated. My arms were empty and nothing would heal that.

Paul and I reacted differently. The funeral was very well attended. The church was packed. Everyone was crying. It felt like a dream. I can't remember whether I cried. I was glad of the nice service. I was glad we were Catholics. At least I would see her again.

Next day, February 4th, Anne gave birth to Mark. I loved him straight away. Anne was devastated at missing the funeral. In fact, she still regrets it.

There is no "right" way to cope. People thought that we were coping. Paul and I had nothing much to say to each other. We needed words but couldn't find them. Josie looked like her dad. They had the same blue eyes.

Paul went back to sea. Dad and the rest of us got up in the morning and existed in-between in that hell called grief and went to bed.

It was difficult for Paul because men don't talk. I had my family. Gill, my best friend. Cousins. Anyone who would listen. Those early weeks were a blur of just existing.

Losing your child is a unique grief. It's a physical grief. I started having panic attacks when I went to Mass. I could see her coffin. I had flashbacks of candle smells, incense and that awful, awful knowledge that after the service comes the cemetery, the grand finale.

I lay awake wondering whether Josie was warm enough in her box; was she missing me too? Did she think that I had abandoned her? You can't leave your child in a box underground and not feel guilty. You can't leave her there and not feel like killing yourself. I wished I were dead so that I could be with her.

I knew that she was with God because I had felt her being physically lifted from me the moment she died. That knowledge was a felt certainty. I stopped going to Mass because of the panic sensations. Claire said it was perfectly normal to feel anxious. It gave me a good excuse. God wasn't my favourite person at this time.

I couldn't say this to anyone. I was afraid to ask, why? Afraid of what, I'm not sure. Being struck down, maybe? I wish!

I have never been one to express my feelings in public. Maybe this was why people thought I was coping. I would get drunk and cry myself to sleep, but only in the privacy of my own bed.

The months passed and the numbness wore off. Enter rage and anger. I hated children who were her contemporaries. She would never to go to play school, sit on the swings, experience life. Yet, other parents paraded their children outside my house. Their lives had been spared and this angered me. The anger strangled me. I wanted to scream "it's not fair". I wasn't perfect but I had coped; a disabled mum, I had looked after her the best way I could.

She was gone and life remained. Her contemporaries

grew up. Why not Josie? She had done nothing wrong. The tortuous anger was killing me. I was totally unprepared for the searching phase.

You look for them in the street. A pram the same colour. You catch a glimpse of the same coat. Relief for a second and then you remember that it is not Josie's coat. Josie's dead. She's in Heaven. She doesn't need a coat. That child you saw wearing a coat like Josie's is alive. She needs a coat.

The searching nearly destroyed me. I kept looking for her. And each time I failed to find her, Josie died a little bit more. I dreamt of her. She was OK. I would wake up convinced that I was dreaming all this hurt. Then I would remember and dread the emptiness that lay before me.

I needed to talk about her. Very few actually listened. Perhaps they couldn't cope. Or perhaps they were too busy. Dad liked the saying, "everyone wants to know, but no-one wants to listen". How true. It's fine while the drama is unfolding, but once it is over only a few stick around.

What is so taboo about mentioning my baby's name? She is mine. I conceived and gave birth to her. She has a birth certificate. I have photos of her. She did exist, you know. I carried her for nine months. I pushed her into this world and she even had a few teeth. Yes, she's dead. Yes, it's unfair but please don't pretend that nothing has happened. Are you afraid of losing your child? Is that why you crossed the road? Is that why you told me that Josie looked yellow?

Does being flippant and cruel hide your deepest fear? I pray that you never experience the loss of your child. Though why should you be spared? It's always the nice ones who get hurt. The rotten ones are left to destroy the feelings of others. The good die young. Where does that leave you, then? Or me come to that.

So clear off. Deny yourself. Pretend I have never been the mother of a dying child. Have you so little courage? I thought you said you loved Jesus Christ. So where were you when my heart was breaking? Cleaning the church? Arranging the flowers? When my eyes were dull, did you not see? Did you pray for us? For me? For Josie? Oh, Josie never existed did she. She was a figment of my imagination. My stretch marks are imaginary. Those aching arms are not empty at all.

How dare you call yourself a Christian? She is in Heaven now. So what! Is that supposed to make things all right? I know she's in Heaven. I felt Him take her away from me.

Let me be the one to own the experience. Don't tarnish my child with your fears and doubts. Go and talk to your Priest. Don't use a small, defenceless dead child to hide behind.

She was my little girl. Ask yourself why you walked away. Then you might be honest enough to see God. Hide behind good works and hours of "doing" and you will be imprisoned. Entombed in an inauthentic faith. Use my pain as an excuse to hide your own and pretend that you are holy.

"You will have another baby," someone said. How cruel. How rude. I should have slapped that person. Nothing replaces a lost child. It is not like losing a set of car keys. She was my life.

Is it that you don't value life, or are you just terrified of your own death? I will ask God to send me ten more children. That should assuage you. Put your mind at ease. Even if I had a hundred children, no-one could replace my little angel.

I can call her that because God entrusted her to us. Are

26

you envious of that? Do you feel put out that you were not chosen by God to carry an angel? Does your ordinariness and unworthiness before God strangle you?

Don't waste my time. You have religion. I have faith. Religion is formal and authoritarian. Faith is a close relationship with God. Bury your child and then dare to shake my hand. Bury your child and we will see how true to God you really are. Don't patronise me with empty condolences.

Watch those scary dark-clothed undertakers carry a tiny coffin. They lower it into a filthy gaping hole in the ground. Chant prayers, parrot-fashion, "eternal rest". And then walk way from your flesh and blood. Squeamish, eh? This is my reality. Josie lost her life. You have still got yours. You still have your child. Mine will never grow up. How does that make you feel? Uneasy? That was Jesus Christ in that ground. This is the cross of Golgotha.

This is why He sent His Son. Have you not understood? What religion have you been practising? A Pharisical one. You cannot be true to our Lord unless you step into our shoes. You can pass useless comments, or say a novena.

"I don't think I could cope," you say. And I can? You must be hard of heart. No-one copes with this. This is every parent's nightmare. This is as tough as it gets.

Keep your clichés. I don't need them. I love my God. Does this surprise you? I have quarrelled with Him. I have bargained with Him. I'll do anything, anything, God, so long as she lives.

I have a right to say this because I am her mother. His Will is not ours, but I can accept it. I have to live with it or be destroyed.

Could you do this? Or would you need valium and antidepressants? That's hard. Take a hard look at your heart and experience what we had to.

Not a happy place. We've been there. We have grappled with the mystery of God. Not because we chose to but because He willed it.

THE CAREFREE TOMBOY

I have fond memories of my early years. Some can recall their first steps and sitting in pushchairs. My memory is poor. I have blocks of amnesia, cruelly and mercilessly filled in by siblings.

Richard was an only child for over eleven years and then came Claire, a much-prayed-for second child. By that time my mother was suffering severe episodes or flare-ups of rheumatoid arthritis. She coped with the help of my father, a new man pushing a pram in the early 60's, and the help of her family. Then, to everyone's delight, came twins. Anne was born three hours before me, in a local cottage hospital two days before Christmas 1961. I was reluctant to enter this world, arriving at Bangor thirty miles away. Everyone said I was the awkward one. The one who would stand in a sweet shop for an hour and emerge with an apple. We were a close family, with the usual sibling rivalry of course.

We were ordinary kids in an ordinary street. Playing catch was an obsession. Anne was placid and shy. Claire spoke for the both of us. Richard helped pick up the pieces. I used to have tantrums and would lash out if confronted or told what to do. Hiding under a table after a misdemeanour. Anne would take the blame.

I loved to play dare. Standing on a chair, reaching for a cherished ornament, "Don't you dare," but I did. I smashed it because I felt like it. I threw Richard's prized possessions downstairs just to annoy him. It worked.

We spent hours on the beach in Pwllheli. The summer holidays lasted forever. Mam used to say that I was the first in the water and the last out. We would take sandwiches and squash and Claire would dig a hole in the sand, find some wood and build a car. She would have to be in the driving seat. Anne never minded much, but I did. I'd get fed up and gather the sand, quickly demolishing the whole show.

Shirley was my best friend at school. We shared everything, including Anne. Cairn Monaghan, a close friend, used to be my tennis partner every June when Wimbledon was re-enacted in a field in town. I loved sports. I loved playing outside. Always on the go.

I was so mean to Anne, I wouldn't let her play with me outside school. Claire kept her company whilst I ran amok. You would go to the corner shop with a list in those days. Getting bits and pieces for Mam. We busied ourselves with our imaginations in those early years. We had a shed in the garden and my mother would keep empty shopping containers and we'd play for hours, until someone got fed up. My parents encouraged reading. Enid Blyton was a favourite. My own daughter Rebecca is an outdoor girl, without my worrying behavioural difficulties.

I suppose I was attention-seeking, though my mother treated us all equally. I used to ask her who was her favourite; she'd smile and say, "I love you all equally but in different ways". Anne understands – she has four children of her own. You love them all, you understand their differing needs and personalities. I wish that Rebecca wasn't an only child. It's not her fault that her sister died. The cousins are more like siblings, probably because our parents have died and we, the parents, have become closer as a result.

I remember those warm striped flannelette sheets. A hot water bottle in the winter. We'd fight over the Baby Belling electric heater, it warmed a little circle in the bed.

After a bath my mother would warm our vests in front of an electric fire. She'd make us a warm drink when we were particularly cold. When we were ill, she'd make a big fuss. Always believing us even if our temperatures weren't life-threatening.

She loved making cakes and cooking our favourites. I'd sit at the table waiting for the roast potatoes. Willing the gas cooker to hurry up. Impatient even then. It gives me pleasure even now when Rebecca and Paul demolish a roast dinner. It's worth every boring hour in the kitchen.

Dad would tell us stories of when he was a little boy. About his father, a baker, and how he used to get up early each day to have breakfast with his dad. His mother would wait up for the children, no matter when they walked in.

It is love that has carried us all through the tough times. I'm convinced of this. My mother hid her illness well. She said we were good children and it made life easier. Love blinded her to my tantrums, evidently. We felt wanted and cherished. Even when we squabbled as the hormones kicked in later on, we were encouraged to make up and told that families stick together, no matter what.

Richard left for University when I was about six and I became pale and withdrawn. I was experiencing separation anxiety even then. I would count the days until he returned with washing and pocket money and tales of college.

Our parents worked hard to provide us with the education they never had. My dad could have been an accountant. Mam wanted to be a teacher. Things were different in those days and that is why we were encouraged to learn. So that we wouldn't have to struggle like they did. Later on, I'd lament my years at college and Dad would say, "No-one can take those degrees away from you". I hope we did them proud.

When we were small, Dad used to work in the Butlins Holiday Camp and we'd have a pass to spend the day there. We would walk for miles visiting the zoo, swimming, eating candy floss and going home tired and happy. With useless toys from an expensive shop and sticks of rock for good measure.

Curiously enough, I was the busiest of the girls. Climbing trees, jumping over barbed wire, fearless and free. I breathed in every experience as if it were my last. I'd fall into bed, exhausted but ready for tomorrow. Dad couldn't understand my insomnia in later life. My head used to grace the pillow and I was always the first to sleep.

Mass was a must. I was allowed out to play before and after. Mam used to say that "an hour is not too much to ask, you can play for the rest of the week". I say the same thing to Rebecca. Tradition is important even today. It gives security and a foundation. We were told to respect authority and to toe the line. Any disagreements or "trouble" was to be resolved within the family. Dad said, "Face the lion head-on and you will find courage". In other words, take responsibility for your actions. Learn from mistakes. Problem-solving, the experts would call it.

Mam had a lot of emotional support from her sisters. Her father died when we were young but Ninnie outlived her eldest daughter. Mam was the eldest girl in the family of seven children. Motherhood came easy to her. She was like a mother to her brothers and sisters. This capacity to love was often taken for granted. But love she did.

Dad used to take us for long walks. I suspect that Mam was catching up with the chores, or resting maybe. We were never at a disadvantage because of her illness. She protected us from that. I know that cost her dearly emotionally. It spared us, which is what she insisted on. We rarely missed any schooling because Mam was ill. She did not let it interfere with our agendas, and I thank her for that.

As a disabled mother myself, I admire her strength of spirit, her courage and her determination to get it right. She did her best. And it was more than good enough. For nothing can undermine that feeling of belonging, of being loved even when you are unlovable. Of being accepted totally. I did not understand that her faith in God was her rock. I'd watch her pray a novena, but I never knew why there was a Sacred Heart picture above her bed. She loved God and His Blessed Mother. Of all the legacies, the greatest was the faith. Because she taught us that compassion and love and faith go hand in hand. She accepted her illness as God's will.

Me, I thought Mass was too long and boring. I used to giggle and fidget and get poked in the back; I didn't care.

It was almost as if I had no conscience. I was never sorry about anything. I had a will of iron. Whether it was sulking or playing, I was aware of a great strength.

I did it all with such passion and willpower. Consequences never occurred to me. I wanted it all now. I breathed life. Running and skipping. Playing hopscotch for hours and hours. I had no limits physically. I always wanted to go that step further. Needed that extra challenge.

In retrospect, although I wasn't diagnosed with JCA until I was ten years old, I think I was developing symptoms much earlier. At about eight years old I remember doing ballet. I was kitted out in the tutu and shiny slippers and I couldn't get up from the floor. I was always pale, yet robust at the same time.

Yes, I had a whale of a time. Children are sometimes diagnosed as young as a few months old. I had a head start in that respect. I enjoyed a normal childhood for those crucial years. I lost it as soon as the diagnosis was confirmed. It broke my mother's heart. My dad's too. I carried on as if nothing had changed. Only it had, and this will of iron was there, only it was targeted at illness rather than at fun and play.

But the battle would be a lifetime's worth. Winning the battle only to lose the war. Thank God I did not understand the concept of incurable at so young an age.

I was the same person, but everything had changed. I still wanted to play. To run and swim. The wants did not go away, but it was beyond my control. Just because you can't have it doesn't mean that you don't want it. Desire and need remain the same, feel the same. That young, carefree tomboy was screaming to get out. It was impossible. The psychological torture was just beginning. Someone had said "no" and Jane was having none of it.

A CHILD'S EYE

Part 1

The symptoms came and went. Some days I was my normal self, but other days were not so good. My feet and hands hurt. I was pale and always tired. My mother recognised the tell-tale signs. She had lived with them for a good part of her life. She must have prayed for a mistake. For a wrong diagnosis. I wish to God I could have spared her this.

Months passed and my GP sent me to a paediatrician. My ESR (the level of inflammation in the blood) was sky high. Rheumatoid factor positive.

I carried on. I had the same "thing" as my mother. This didn't kill you. So what? She was alive.

The beauty of innocence and a mind that cannot grasp. Of doors that had been closed before they had opened. Opportunities missed before they had been dreamed of. My life was over, the one I had lived before. The fun tomboy was lost. But I couldn't let her go and I hung on this denial for more than twenty years.

My mother insisted that I was extra special. That God had chosen me. I didn't care. Anger was healthier than acceptance but I could not give this feeling a face, a name or shape. I was no longer myself and yet I could not be anyone else.

Something felt different deep inside and a battle was starting. My physical self had taken over. The innocent soul was just about to emerge and mature and I crushed it, ignored it, forbade it to speak to me. I could not see beauty and love and life because I was ashamed of the way I walked. Ashamed of pain and the manifestations of arthritis. I felt old and grey and I'd only just entered puberty. Everything was pushed back into my subconscious mind and the mask was truly planted onto a face that cried only behind curtains. I became a comedienne, to the outside world at least. At home I was your average moody hormonal teenager. I worked hard at school because I wanted to achieve something and my brains were as good as the rest. I would compete intellectually but that's all. Boys and discos were out. Inpatient appointments, sterile needles, intimidating surgeons were in. I felt trapped between two selves. I was Jane and the arthritis thing was separate. But it wasn't. It was me. I never connected. I was two people. They must never become one. That would be unthinkable. Like sitting in a therapy session, saying "I'm Jane, and I've got arthritis". No way – this was a long, long way off.

My mother wanted me to accept this but I couldn't. Mothers and daughters are supposed to share shopping trips, not hospital appointments. We had to see the same Rheumatologist. Go through the same system that labels you and scribbles notes about you. Only they don't know me. They don't know my mother. She's not crippled. She's my Mam and she looks after us all. So what the hell are we doing sitting in a Rheumatology clinic, both of us far too young, far too busy protecting and colluding? She had God. I didn't want anyone.

Not the doctors or the endless GP visits and the rubbish that came with this hot inflammation that was ravaging my young body. I blocked it out. Psychologically that is. I couldn't ignore the fire in my feet. My hands slowly twisting. The loss of tasks long learnt. I watched my mother, as if for the first time, and saw my future self. Would I be like all these other nameless crippled numbers, I asked, as my eyes roamed the endless round of pale and defeated faces. I'm not really here. I'm accompanying my mother, and that's bad enough. She doesn't deserve this. She's not like those people. Where's Jane then? I've left her at home. I'm someone else. A teenager that's here but shouldn't be. I'm someone whose joints are corroding so fast that the surgeons are called in.

X-rays taken, blood cross-matched. Getting closer to the first major hip replacement. Only I'm too young they say. Jane says nothing. Jane's at home, perfectly normal and walking like a ballerina. I was dangerously outside myself and yet blissfully unaware of the dangers and the cost of such faulty thinking.

Curiously, I passed my 'O' Levels and maintained relationships. I wore the latest fashions and fell in love with Hutch from "Starsky and Hutch". I had a crush on a sixth former and experimented with eye kohl and foundation. But this other girl, the one with arthritis, kept getting in the way and the pain was eating away inside. Unfairness, envy was what I felt as I watched the others do games. Walk tall. Walk without pain.

The teachers were great, especially Gwyneth Sol Owen, my English teacher and Dewi Williams, the History teacher. They seemed to understand, and I was interested in these subjects. Counselling was not an option in those days. I lost myself in books and exams, had a lot of time off school and plenty of support too.

This schizophrenic-style psyche was a necessary and useful tool. I was unable to cope with the psychological nature of a chronic condition, crippling me bit by bit, and I felt betrayed and bitter and sad. Expressing emotion was not the done thing in those days. I tried to keep walking, following doctors' orders, but the disease raged on until two major joints needed replacing. This is inflammatory arthritis at its worst. I couldn't stop it. I couldn't stop it crippling my mother. I hated the mere mention of arthritis, although Mam and I jokingly called it "Arthur".

It wasn't funny and I wasn't laughing; outwardly stoic, I resented this beast that travelled through my blood.

Someone had betrayed me, but I didn't know who or how to blame. I couldn't blame the God my mother loved so much. If anyone mentioned hereditary, I would jump to my mother's defence. It is not hereditary. We were the only two. I should think that two was more than sufficient.

I ended up blaming myself. Intellectually, this was nonsensical but someone had to pay for all this pain and torment – and what better defence than self-blame? I must have done something wrong. Sure, I broke ornaments and flew into rages, but I didn't deserve this. As I became consciously aware of life and its offerings, I began to feel out of place. I was normal and I wasn't.

It's like watching black-and-white TV when the set is in faint colour. Like looking into a shop window and not being able to buy. It's like that sinking sensation when you're not chosen for the lead part – only this feeling stays with you.

Here's the world but you can't have me. You are disabled. You can't have the cream doughnut. You must make do with a jam one. No cream for you. You are different although you pretend that you are not.

You have to be able to walk to participate. Didn't you know that only the strongest survive? They'll spit you out no matter how much you want acceptance – it's not here. In the real world. It's not here!

Low self-esteem, according to experts, is caused by a lack of unconditional love. It doesn't fit. I was loved and cherished. I had a listening mother who stayed at home and made cakes. This lack of confidence was all around me in the schoolyard. I couldn't see this. I didn't know that you could be an emotional cripple. How could I? These dilemmas went on in the subconscious, so deep and so hidden that it took me years to work it out.

I was one voice, not two. Self-talking was a necessary mechanism. I had so little control over my body and my life choices. Everything seemed so complicated and painful. So I shut off. The arthritis had won, for now at least.

Let it savage my growing body. See if I care! Do your worst and spit me out. Eat my joints, take my blood. When asked by those in white coats, I would say I was fine. Only test results tell a tale. X-rays tell the truth. I don't care. Take everything, you can have the inside of me if you can find it. No, hang on. I don't know what or where it is but you can't have that. Its mine. The blood can't destroy that. And neither can you. It was my soul and I was damned if I was giving that away. They can't steal it. I won't let them.

Evidently, the medical profession, over the delicate growing up and evolving years, became public enemy number 1. I was polite enough, quite funny when I wanted to be, but I was fed up of parading like a performing monkey. Only to be told that this was wrong and that needed putting right.

I was tired of being controlled. They'd all gather on ward

rounds, discuss, smile and shake their heads. Later on they would return. With cortiosteroid injections, neck collars and a list of dos and donts. I didn't know about side effects. I bled in my stomach once. No-one told me why. I didn't ask because I was scared. I only knew when units of blood arrived and colour came back to my cheeks.

The Rheumatology field has made great strides since those days. They did their best. Gobowen Hospital is a leading hospital. I knew I was well cared for. I just insisted I wasn't there. It was nobody's fault. They were very kind. Psychological effects were secondary. They had to keep me mobile. With traction, sticks, hydrotherapy and so on. I wore this horrendous knee brace, like something out of the Middle Ages, in a vain and desperate bid to straighten my left knee. We had a laugh when I squeaked walking, stiff and pale and weary. Only all I felt was shame and indignation. I couldn't understand my feelings.

So I played the clown. The bionic woman passing her exams. Denying that I was damaged far deeper than the physical scarring. I didn't want to upset anyone. I couldn't find expressions. Scared of the dark side of myself I feared that these thoughts would bury me alive. So I kept them to myself.

This "thing" would not get the better of me. I was not going to let it stop me. I planned to be a social worker. Hardly the occupation for the immobile. I planned anyway. Determined to go away to college, defying doctors' orders, I was going to live and show them they were wrong. Prove to them that I was not a statistic. The anger was keeping me afloat. Anger is a wonderful motivator. It feels red and hot. It made me right and everybody else wrong. Anger empowered me. I believed that I had given it away. I reclaimed it with a tight mouth and gritted teeth. Pain makes you angry, loss of independence makes you cringe. Lack of understanding is the hardest to bear. Lack of compassion. Patronizing gazes. A pat on the shoulder. Jane, the hero. Big deal. I ain't no hero. That's my mother. Jane's not ill. She bears the physical manifestations of a chronic illness but she's fine now, thanks. She's okay, really she is.

The anger is mine. You can't see it. I bet you don't even know it's there. Ha ha! No X-ray will show you what I really think of all this. It's my secret. My friend. Anger feels strong and big. It can cover up all that you want to see but can't. Anger gives you energy and a quest for the impossible. I will reach the stars. I will find a cure. I will not be like this for the rest of my life. I won't let it happen to me. I'll be different. I believed the angry voice. It was the only one I had. It was my secret weapon and we worked well as a team.

I did not know that anger destroys. Anger is futile. Negative and self-perpetuating. Anger hurts you twice. It achieves nothing except momentary release. A fragile tent to hide under. I did not care. It suited me fine. I'll hang on to this because I can't feel anything else. It will have to do. It's all I've got. And they can't touch it.

A CHILD'S EYE

Part 2

The psychological trauma of a chronic juvenile disability is carried on into adulthood in a distressing and unnecessary way. Because the child cannot say "no" and can't tell them when to stop. The powerlessness is crushing for the child who wants to please and then gets hurt. "We are here to help you," and then a doctor comes with a large needle and someone helps him to take your pants down and in goes the injection. You try not to cry and tug at your modesty hoping that no-one was looking. It would have been nice to have been asked.

If you knew what humiliation was, then this is what you would call it. Young children don't have the words, but the pain is the same. If you could give it expression, then few would do justice to the unrelenting and excruciating pain of juvenile rheumatoid arthritis.

My mother, a woman of great courage with a faith to match, used to say that God does not give you more than you can bear. I disagreed with her and she would warn me of the perils of blasphemy.

When you are so small and alone in a strange hospital the fear stays with you. They give orders, and every ounce of specimen they take, they take away from you. That small child can never get back what has been lost.

I screamed at my mother for leaving me in a hospital "for

babies". She could barely walk herself. Her arthritis was playing up, but all I could feel was abandonment. All I could feel was anger and resentment.

I couldn't articulate my feelings. So I cried and tugged at her skirt whilst her heart was breaking. I cringe now when I think of how she felt, but I was barely eleven years old. How it must have hurt her to leave me there and then go home on the bus. Carrying home these painful recollections and probably blaming herself. She had to take extra pills to do the work after she got home. The arthritis probably acted up more because of the stress of having a child with the same horrible disease. That didn't make me feel good, having to worry about her when she was ill herself.

Finding the bathroom is difficult in a strange hospital. I never knew which way to go. I felt lost and angry at being dragged here in the first place. I knew where the bathroom was at home. Why don't they leave me alone?

Anger to a young child means showing hurt by tantrums and throwing things, kicking doors and using that big word that grown ups don't like. But in hospital you can't do that. You have to be polite and thank them when they have finished hurting you. And still more anger as the injection burns when they said it wouldn't.

Then when you go home you're a bit of a hero until they leave you to play bikes and hopscotch. And you have to stand and watch with tears burning behind your eyes. But you daren't let them see. It's bad enough being different without being called a cry-baby as well.

Time for clinic and a dodge from school. The teachers don't believe I've got an old person's disease but my mum's written them a note. My friends don't like it because I can skip games, but I would gladly swap with them. I would swap all this pain for a game of hockey. But they don't understand and neither do I. But I've got my first bra so I'm nearly part of the gang. A white bra with red roses on it. I'm almost normal. I didn't know that this was self-consciousness. Modesty, or lack of it. Prodded and poked and not allowed to express myself. Looking at my mam to see if she would understand what they said about my feet and hands and legs. The long words meant nothing to me then. All I knew was that I was tired and achey and stiff. I thought that it would clear up and then maybe it would come back when I was older and it was time.

I can't recollect the exact moment when I ceased to be a child. Somewhere, and well before it was time, laughter died and the fun and the freedom ebbed away. Something precious had been lost to me and I never even knew it. That feeling of aliveness had gone. When you jump over a fence and don't worry if you've left your trousers behind. The vibrancy of playing catch with a tennis ball for hours and hours without getting tired. The glowing anticipation of a child's eye and the spontaneity of choice. And you can't mourn because you don't know that there has been a bereavement. And you can't cry because you don't think that you've got a right to.

No-one told me that to cry was a sign of weakness but I decided, as young as eleven years of age, to be strong. Burying my feelings and disappointments under a burden of agony that I never fully learnt how to express. I'd always been a bit of a tomboy and would think nothing of throwing ornaments around when my sisters got in the way. I threw Richard's wireless downstairs – he was twelve years older than me – and, worryingly, I showed no remorse. I wanted it all yesterday.

44

Subconsciously I hid a great deal in order to spare my mother. Not that I thought that her needs came before mine, or that she was more worthy. I knew that this was hurting them too although it was unexpressed. Indeed, Mam told me many times that I was her main concern and that she had had her life and the dancing and the carefree days of youth. She was very unselfish. Both my parents were. They must have agonised in those hours after we had gone to bed. Where does this need to protect come from? How can a young girl decide, whether consciously or subconsciously, to put on an act and pretend that nothing is different?

My life had changed, for post-diagnosis everything was "You can't". "You musn't." "Be careful, Jane." Until I wanted to kick and scream. The doctors never looked at me when they were talking, it was as if they were discussing someone else. No-one asked me how I felt, only how I was. It was easier to say "Fine, thanks," and leave it at that. The less they enquired, the bigger my defence grew.

The concept of disability is intriguing because no-one actually confirms that you are disabled, you just "feel" different because there are so many things that you cannot do. I didn't feel disabled until I started noticing boys, and although nobody called me a cripple I felt like one. Because I had a stick. It hurts like that moment in your teens when you suddenly look in the mirror and you realise that you don't look like a film star. Right up to the last moment of puberty there is hope. You've stopped feeling so you don't know how you feel and nobody asks, so it can't really matter. If it did, someone would want to know; someone would ask.

Children with chronic illnesses enter into an adult arena, a place where children shouldn't have to go. A battlefield where no child should enter. Many do, though, and I knew that there were children far worse off than I was. This should have made me feel better, but I'm not sure that it did.

Logically, maybe, but not emotionally. It is necessary to divorce yourself from emotion because it would have been too overwhelming. The sense of frustration ate into my very soul. It is far safer to fantasise then to cope with reality. Only you don't realise that fantasy is not the reality and vice versa. While my defence mechanism is intact, things can run fairly smoothly, as what you cannot feel cannot hurt; you block with the biggest bricks hoping that the facade won't crumble. Because if it does you may well be destroyed.

The true concept of pain eludes most people because it is a sign of things being wrong and they immediately demand to get rid of it. Very early on, before I understood what it meant, I knew what it felt like. Instinctively, I felt that others were uncomfortable with pain. It wasn't as if it was there to be uncomfortable with, but they winced when I told them the gory details. They stopped asking and I stopped telling.

I got angry when they didn't understand and I got angry when they didn't want to know. I'm not sure that I would want to know if it was happening to them. Why do people insist on finding me a cure when I know there isn't one? They want to cure me to make themselves feel better, to absolve themselves maybe. So that they don't feel guilty for having good health and so they don't feel awkward about being able to walk properly when I can't. In essence, they are transferring their non-understanding onto me and I don't want it.

GRIEF UNMEASURED AND UNCONSOLED

At 7.40 a.m. on Sunday, October 13th, 1985, I woke to the desperate voice of my father calling out "Molly, Molly!" No answer. Nothing. I knew. I don't know how, but I knew that she was dead.

The GP said something about a blood clot. Sudden death. "Mam, wake up, don't do this to me. To us. It's not time, God." The picture of the Sacred Heart above their bed looked down at me. "You've got it wrong, God." I couldn't stop shaking. Anne was as white as a sheet. My dad was pacing up and down and the light had gone out of our lives. She was only 60. Richard, her eldest, was abroad and Claire, her much-longed-for second child, was working in London.

Downstairs, on the gas cooker, were the dried peas and pork chops. Pathetic, useless reminders of today's Sunday roast. Only there will be no dinner. Only shock, disbelief and tears. She's dead.

There are voices downstairs. Maybe someone can tell me it's not true. Devastated aunties, incessant phone calls.

My grandmother, her mother, tucked her in like a small child. Pulling the covers up one last time before the gruesome realities of embalming and undertakers. The Hail Marys were chanted, and this new business of dying had penetrated our walls as well as our souls.

Sudden death brings complications. Why? What happened to her? Could we have done something? It is too late now. No time for paramedics. Our Lord took her in her sleep.

Later that Sunday, exhausted and raw, I saw her in her coffin. She wasn't my mother. The smell of wood and candles and flowers in our front room was the smell of death. Separation. Someone has been snatched. Well before time. Experts believe that viewing the body helps us to accept the reality and finality, but I'm not sure. It frightened me to death. I know it's my mother in that box, but it doesn't look like her, or feel like her, and it hurts like hell.

Reality is pork chops in the dustbin, her clothes still hanging and her handbag beside the bedside cabinet. Reality is a pension book that has to be returned to the authorities, tablets that are no longer needed and a family that does not know what to do.

I must be dreaming. This is not happening. We were laughing yesterday. She was regaining her mobility after a complicated hip replacement. She had planned today's meal and here she is in that horrible coffin. Oh God, Mam, where are you? Don't go, I've got things to tell you. Joyce and Stephen's wedding yesterday. We had a good night, Mam. You must not die. You haven't seen this baby. I never told you that you are the best mother in the world. Please wake up. You can die when I have finished loving you. Not now, please. I never said thank you. Dear Lord in Heaven, tell me that this is a dream. She can't die now. I can't handle this. Everyone is devastated. Don't die – not yet!

A dose of heparin could have saved her. Love so unconditional silenced by a blood clot. The warm, tender, compassionate heart has stopped beating and she is lying in the front room.

The life kicking inside me makes a mockery of the death

in the parlour. I don't want a baby. I want my mother.

There is a hole where my heart should be. My chest is burning with shock and unshed tears. I want to scream. Kick something. Our cat, Kiki, comes into the window to remind me of the living. Dad won't have her in the house. He sits, trying to be brave and fooling no-one.

The undertaker is talking about closing the box. Don't. It's too final. I'll never see her again. I heard the screws closing. The final nail. That's my mam in there. Don't lock her in. She can't get out. Don't be so cruel. She's our mother, not a body. You've just broken my heart; leave the lid open, don't close it. I can feel the panic rising. This is real. Those nails are real. Show some respect. He's only doing his job. He's just encased Mam in a horrible pine box and I can think what I bloody well want.

The funeral was well attended; hymns, reading, didn't hear or see much. I stuck to my dad hoping to give him strength. My aunties made a beautiful buffet arrangement. How grateful we were. We clung to one another, hoping to amass a strength. Courage, conviction that she was in Heaven.

I felt her absence most in our kitchen. The empty chair. I could hear her struggling footsteps. It can't be you, but I can hear you still. My mind was racing, going over the last conversations. Silence. No-one answers your grief. No-one hears the scream. The emptiness. The futility of longing for someone and the brutality of having to accept that death is irreversible. You can't bring them back. Regardless of how much you have loved, death is final. This is a nightmare, and we have to live through it. And God knows this.

I feel orphaned. How could you leave me? Were you so tired that you took Our Lord's hand when He called? I don't blame you. You didn't have to die to have a rest. Death was too drastic. Who's going to help me with this baby when it comes? I'm lost, drowning, I need your skirt to cling to, your small but strong hand to hold onto. I need you to tell me that everything will be alright.

Remember when I was ill, home from school, I had you all to myself. I felt so loved, so safe and wanted. Didn't you want us any more? Was it too hard to carry on? You should have said. We could have made it better. You didn't have to die! Claire, Anne, Richard, Dad and all of us, we don't know what to do. We haven't got a map. The grief is strangling us and everything has lost its colour.

Your disability aids are still here. I hate them. You hated them too. They stare at me, mockingly. You have no need for them now. Things have no meaning because you aren't here to use them. The Social Services will probably want them back now. Does anybody care except us? Why are they expecting us to get back to normal? They speak of buying presents for their mums for Christmas. All we'll have is a graveyard and a bunch of flowers.

If you could return for just one day, Mam. I would give you the whole world. Cook your favourite meal, buy you a fine dress. Make coffee the way you liked it, milky and hot.

I'm sorry about the tantrums. The times I took you for granted. Seeing you struggle with arthritis and looking away because I couldn't bear to see you suffer. I could have helped more around the house. I wish I had listened to your stories about your days in the Wrens. How you met Dad and the early years. I'll never know now. It's too late. So many questions left.

I go to bed thinking that the cloud of grief will lift, but I wake up with that empty pit in my stomach. I look for you in your bedroom. Your pillows remain untouched. You don't sleep here anymore. And it hurts so much that I wish I could join you. But Dad needs me. Paul needs me and so does my unborn child.

I thought that everyone loved in the way that you did. Without conditions or agendas. I was wrong and my heart became bitter.

I did not know that people could be so dismissive and distant. Cold. Busyness is no excuse for ignoring the hurt and the bereaved. I was bewildered and aghast at the "at least she went in her sleep" brigade. Oh wow, I really feel consoled!

I want you to make a roast dinner for me. I want to be that little girl sitting on your knee. Stroking your warm face. I miss being someone's daughter. Someone's little girl. "At least she didn't suffer," they said. Excuse me. She suffered for years and years. Taking painkillers to cook the tea. Fastening the nappies with her teeth because her hands were crippled with arthritis. She accepted what you find impossible. Immobility. The loss of freedom of choice. Barely able to do the shopping. Why should you care? Go on, knit for your grandchildren. Give your kids a break when they are tired. Forget about Molly's girls. They don't need mothering. They don't need the benefits of wisdom and advice on raising children. They can cope.

I would cry for her with that gut-wrenching silent wail, "Maaaaaaaaaaaam". As if by calling for her she would come. She would if she could. I know she would. An empty echo. A scream silenced by lack of positive regard. A desperate wanting for that love that only a mother can give. Tell me where you are, Mam, so that I can find you. Only she never came. She couldn't come because she was dead. But that did not stop the yearning. The searing pain in the heart that was becoming more bitter every day.

This emotional turmoil went on and on. Far worse than any physical pain I had experienced. This one pierced my soul. It was irreversible. God had stolen her and the injustice, the sheer unfairness, was crushing.

My spiritual search had begun. The constant argument with the ever present Omnipotent One. A seed had been sown. Remembering her words, "God is good" and "ask Our Blessed Lady" rang in my ears.

Her little novena cards, unused in her handbag. If she believed in God in spite of all the suffering then there must be something in this "Our Lord" business. It made no sense. I thought he'd let her down. I was intrigued. Her suffering had to make sense. Her death had to have meaning before we went mad with the grief. How could she believe in a God who had hurt her? Made her ill?

And if He was so wonderful, why had He left us bereft? Abandoned. Why was our grief so unconsoled, and where were God's disciples? Those who were meant to console the bereaved. Be there. Absorb our hurts when we obviously needed a mum.

He left us like that so that we would seek Him and Him alone. If He had sent a "replacement" we would not have cried out in the darkness. He had to take away all the props so that we could "die" in order to live fully in His love.

I know that now. Fifteen years on. I thank God for a mother so tender and compassionate. A little saint. She carried her cross and told me to carry mine. God would step in. My mother's name was Mary. She has earned her place in Heaven. Thank God for her love, her life, her everything!

MY DAD

I had my first hip replacement when I was eighteen. My quality of life was zero. Life had not been easy as my hip was corroded and I was desperate to go to college. Having missed so much schooling, I barely scraped my 'A' levels with a B in English and C in History. I wanted to live a normal life. I demanded it.

My first hip replacement was a great success. However, in 1990, it began to fail. Rebecca was about two years old and my miracle replacement needed what they call "revision" surgery. In September 1991, I was admitted to Gobowen Hospital. I was twenty-nine years old and terrified. What if I died under the anaesthetic? I had responsibilities at home.

Dr Ward, now deceased, was right to be cautious. It took at least five hours of delicate surgery to remove the old hip. Knocking the old cement out and grafting bone from the bone bank. Someone died of a heart attack just as I was experiencing that warm, sinking, pre-med feeling. I was worried about his family. The nurse turned my head away and said "You shouldn't have to see this, Jane".

I woke up in the recovery room and asked someone to ring home to let Dad and Paul know that I was still alive. Paul's heart was in his boots; he'd lost his job and did not want to worry me. My left side felt as if it was on fire. Heavy and cumbersome. Drips and bottles of blood were everywhere and the morphine shots were very welcome.

I had lost a lot of blood and things had been more complicated. After two major operations and giving birth to two children, I was used to the indignities of bad pain and bedbaths. Every time someone moved me I felt a searing pain on my right side. Something must be wrong. It wasn't as bad as this last time.

I drifted in and out of consciousness. I couldn't pass water and had to be catheterised. I hated those hands touching my raw flesh. In a morphine-induced haze, I pulled the drain out and tried to get out of bed! Luckily no damage was done.

I though of my mother. We had heparin injections to prevent blood clots. I felt guilty that I was receiving treatment that could have saved her life.

Paul had been warned not to bring Rebecca to see me. My face was deathly pale, I was tearful with the pain and I did not want her to see me. Having to stay in bed for seven days was terrible. I felt trapped, annoyed and helpless. I would listen to George Michael tapes and think sorrowful thoughts. God, it hurts. It can't have been a success.

The surgeon, an eminent Professor, assured me that the pain was due to the banging and hammering involved in the operation. I'd been trussed up like a turkey.

The catheter caused an infection. I had to take antibiotics and orange stuff for constipation. The latter caused a stir on the ward. I didn't "go" for seven days. The ensuing inevitable indignity of a suppository caused bouts of laughter. By day eight I awaited the verdict with a sinking inevitability. The curtains were drawn, the deed was done and it gave everyone a laugh.

When the physios got me out of bed the ground came up to meet me. I took deep breaths and persevered. The pain was excruciating. At least I was out of bed. I was not allowed to bear any weight for three months. The crutches were cumbersome and my shoulders ached. I had a long way to go.

The helplessness during my bed rest taught me not to take walking for granted. I had to learn how to walk all over again. Regaining mobility and overcoming the problem of pain made me think about God. I was wheeled to a church service one Sunday morning. My heart was beginning to melt. I had been nursed, bathed, injected and poked. My soul was awakening to the wonderful mystery of where God was in this powerlessness. It was in the care and compassion of the doctors and staff. My search for meaning was taking root.

After three weeks I was allowed home and it was difficult for the first few weeks. I couldn't lift my little daughter Rebecca on my knee. I had been warned not to walk without crutches – but six weeks post-op I walked unaided. Anne was with me and she was sworn to secrecy. I did it! I was cooking with a crutch in one hand and the free one concocting culinary delights.

Paul was going to train for a nursing career. Everyone was settled. It had been hard, but we were on the up.

But on February 13, my father died of a massive stroke. Two days before this I had a short story published. He was over the moon. Then I had a positive pregnancy test. Dad wanted me to have a boy. I was to call him John after two of his war mates. One Wednesday 12th I went to my Aunty Philomena's house. We talked over old times and I came home about midnight. Dad was in the kitchen, feeling unwell. We joked about things and I thought he'd picked up a bug.

He went to bed promising to call me in the night if he needed anything. He thanked me for everything. I kissed him, told him not to be daft and we went to bed.

I heard him call me, "Jane, Jane," around three o'clock in the morning. I jumped out of bed and he had collapsed on the landing. Paul woke up and stayed with him while I called the GP.

Dad, my whole life, the mainstay of the family since Mam's passing, was in serious trouble. He was afraid of disturbing Rebecca. Thinking of someone else at his biggest battle since El Alamein.

Dad, my hero, the Normandy veteran, was having a cerebral haemorrhage. He pushed me against the wall. I banged my head, held his hand and told him we'd be fine once Dr Caradog came. I reassured him: "It's okay, help is coming, you'll be fine. I'm here, Dad." It was hopeless.

The ambulancemen carried him out of the house. I went into the ambulance with him. He was already dead and I was still talking to him. Telling him everything was going to be okay.

Paul went to fetch Anne and her three small children. David, her husband, was on his way home from Manchester. Claire's in-laws were down and we gathered again for that ghastly scenerio. Why was it always our family? The third coffin in six years. Had everyone else been untouched?

Rebecca woke up and watched *Dumbo* on the video. Claire fed the children and once more visitors came and went. Dad came home that night. He looked the perfect gentleman in his best suit. A favourite joke of his came to my mind, about a man lying in state and the ladies were saying how well he looked. "Yes, those two weeks in

Llandudno did him the power of good."

Dad, the funny, kind, compassionate peacemaker had gone to see my mother. He looked peaceful. Father Jones came to say the prayers. Although Dad was a Baptist, he wanted a funeral mass at St Joseph's. He wanted to be in the same church as Mam. He had spoken with Father at great length. I'm grateful to Father Jones for granting him his last request.

The church was packed. I was shaking like a leaf. A nervous exhaustion had seeped in. Anne looked as if she was going to collapse. She was so gaunt and thin. Claire, the eldest girl, tried to be strong for us. Richard was devastated. He had phoned Dad the day before to tell him that he was now a Major in the British Army. How proud he had made Trooper Pierce of the Eighth Army!

We were well versed in the grief experience. The Council Offices where he had worked closed down for his funeral. It was packed with all those he had helped. He was admired for his perserverence and courage. He worked all his life despite having lost his right arm in Normandy. He was a man of the people, champion of the underdog. His funeral told the story. They paid their respects to this simple, ordinary and extraordinary man.

I went to Claire's house on the night of the funeral. I didn't want to go home. I could see no light in his bedroom and I couldn't stand what that meant so I went to my Aunty Phil's house. She was wonderfully kind.

I kept peeling too many potatoes. Dad's not here now. I overestimated the shopping. He liked his tea with real tea leaves like he'd had in the army. How I'd cursed the mess the tea leaves made! I would do anything now to have that mess back again.

Washing up one night, a couple of days after the funeral, I looked out of the window and I knew that I would never again see him walk down that road. There was no disbelief this time. No kidding myself that it was a mistake. He was gone. I didn't have to cook for him ever again. No need to iron his shirts. No need to wait up for him on his nights out.

Outside the home, everyone behaved like they had after my mother and Josie. It was no different. Only there was no Dad to make everything alright.

Thank God, Richard took care of the legalities. Our children were small. We had no time for self-pity. We carried on because we had to. Because he would have wanted us to.

Rebecca, three and a half, took it badly as we had lived with Dad. I said, "Taid's gone to Heaven". A few weeks later, she broke down on the stairs and said "I want Taid".

We cuddled and cried and I made us both a hot drink.

Gill, my best friend, was kind to us. She knew how much I had come to depend on Dad for emotional support. We had shared the financial side of things. Paul was missing him too. I pushed him away. I was carrying our third child but I could not get rid of the anger that our house seemed to be where everyone died.

Dad was a stickler for routine. Paul's life, and mine, had revolved around his routine. Now I could do as I pleased. There was a bitter-sweet freedom here. I felt guilty and lost. I missed our chats. During my long convalescence after the hip replacement, Dad and I spent many hours chatting. As if it was meant to be. He had seen all our children, except little Rachel, Anne's new baby.

Dad had grown in stature after recovering from the shock of losing both my mother and "Josie bach," as he called her.

Far from sitting in the corner and bemoaning his lot, he became a tower of strength. He became both mother and father to us.

He used to get the *Daily Express* and fresh eggs on a Thursday morning at a local shop. His routines made it hard for me to let go. He used to share a taxi from the Conservative Club every Tuesday and Friday night.

I'd stay up, waiting for that taxi, but Dad never came home. I was very bitter. We were orphaned. Everyone else, or so it seemed, had both parents. Why us? Why them?

Silence. Anguish. Each time I was pregnant someone died. On March 31st, twelve weeks into my pregnancy, I began to bleed. I wanted this baby so much. Paul and I wanted a brother or sister for Rebecca. I was convinced it was a boy and he would be called John after Dad's friends who never made it home.

I lost that baby. Losing people was a part of life by now. I was just waiting for my mind to go. A breakdown wasn't far away. I had a D & C, was told they were very sorry and I came home to a clean house, fresh flowers but no dad and no baby. It was only seven weeks since he'd died.

The usual "clichés". The baby was not meant to be. Better now than after it was born, they said. I knew that. I'd buried one child. How dare they be so insensitive? So cruel? Did anybody stop for a moment and wonder what it was doing to us? To me?

Everything that I touched was disintegrating. I felt that as if by being on the scene I was somehow responsible. I wasn't, of course, it just felt as if I was.

For years, I had buried emotional and physical pain. The anger and bitterness grew bigger and bigger. I was not aware of this stone in my heart. Lord, I hid it well.

I almost convinced myself that the nightmares had not occurred. I never had the hysteria – or what I now call a normal emotional response. I barely cried unless it was under the duvet. Why? Who was I protecting? As a family, we regrouped like a pack of animals. A basically human and necessary act. We were talking about the dead people but not convinced that there were really gone. We kept them alive by talking about them. To stop saying their names would seem like instant death. For them and us. Only they were already dead. I just didn't believe it. My logical conscious brain had seen and understood. My heart was unable to cope with so much in so little time.

I did not know where to begin. I wanted to cry, but the tears would not come. Besides the losses, I was in daily chronic pain. I had not come to terms with my illness (God knows, I thought I had) and the clinics and appointments still carried on. I didn't care anymore. I loved Paul and Rebecca, my family, but I felt as if I was running away from something. Or someone. I was too scared to tell God – to utter such blasphemy. I got up in the morning, existed, interacted well enough for people not to worry, and hardly slept. I was tired and ill.

Grief is very much a physical experience. My denial had to be maintained at all costs. It was easier. The loss of my child, our child, and both my parents was too much. The anxiety increased. They were wonderful parents. Enduring difficult circumstances in life, accepting them and turning them into something good.

Dad always wanted an education for his children. They scrimped and saved for us to gain the 'A' levels and degrees. Going without to give us a better start in life. There is a tendency to idolize the dead, but these two were a formidable combination. Gentle and strong. Warm, honourable human beings.

I still clung to the rosary but I was quite lukewam. Rebecca went to school and I began to read. Susan bought books on Carmelite spirituality. I read and read. Something beautiful was starting, but my heart was too hard. God had not began to do His work. He knew that. I wasn't ready. You cannot love and serve Him with a heart of stone.

I could only begin to love Him as my father once I had learnt to let go of my anger and grief. It took a major drug problem and four years of counselling for this change to come about. Without this humiliating addiction problem, I would still be lost. In denial, hiding behind net curtains. Blaming everybody else. Anger eating away at me. Without the tranquiliser problem I would not have dropped my defence. I would not have lived fully and humanly.

Dads are strong and protective and they guard against whatever beckons.

We had faced catastrophic losses and he became a rock. Had our mother not died first, I would never have known how much of a humanitarian my father was. Stereotypically, dads are in the background providing financial stability and defending whatever needs defending. He became much more than our father when he lost his wife. He somehow increased in stature and was not diminished by grief. He demonstrated an inner strength and courage possessed only by those who value life.

It took a long time for him to handle my mother's death and little Josie's too. I turned to him for guidance on managing such emotions and in his own way he told me that we just had to get through it or go mad. I'm not sure how a top psychologist would perceive this grief reation.

What about the stages of grief, and so on? My father had seen too much in the war to ponder on PTSD. He was an expert. He had survived and moved on. This was my parents' greatest legacy to us. As harsh as it sounds, the amateur psychologist was right. We had to exist and stick together as a family. Drawing comfort and strength from whoever had anything to give.

His mother, Sydney Jane, was a major influence in his life. Warm and motherly, and always available, her death had a profound effect on him. She died on Boxing Day and he was somewhat morose and reflective on her anniversary. He spoke fondly of his father, a baker, and of getting up early to share breakfast with him. These anecdotes were recounted decades later and his background of unconditional love shaped him.

Dad was a fine diplomat. Family came first, no matter what. There was the usual bickering, fallings out over daft things, and then quickly reconciling or agreeing to disagree. Dad taught by example. He treated everyone the same. He had nothing to prove. He had the medals. There was no need for boasting. The respect his friends and colleagues had for him was apparent. His sense of humour and the ability to turn the negative into something good was formidable.

My intense analysing used to puzzle him. He was very black-and-white in his views and we argued over current affairs and morality.

You reap what you sow. I did not look after him out of a sense of duty and he never expected us to move in with him. We loved him and it was the most natural thing to do. Perhaps I needed to be needed. Maybe I needed his reassurance and strength more than he needed my practical skills, such as they were. His regimental routines drove me crazy and yet they gave order amidst the chaos and search for truth. He believed in an afterlife and had no fear of dying. His worst nightmare was losing the power in his one remaining arm. A loss of independence and control that would ensure that the "disabled daughter" would not be able to cope. He would voice these fears and we would make light of them. It was an unspoken promise that, whatever it took, his children would not let him down. He would threaten to join the Chelsea Pensioners when I had burnt the pork chops. A reluctant cook, maybe, but loyal nonetheless.

Paul took a back seat for six years. Such was his regard for the war veteran, he has since said that he would not change a thing.

You can't force someone to love you. You have to earn that respect. Dad was kind and funny and honourable. He could be grumpy, old fashioned and irritatingly right. But he was my father.

He prepared me for his death in a joking, "What will you do when I'm gone?" way; the thought terrified me and he'd laugh. Telling me that we all have to "go" when it's time. Previous losses don't prepare you for the next one. His sudden passing was devastating. In the same way as my mum's. Six years on and he'd gone to meet her. I loved them both equally and mourned their loss in equal measure. I still miss my mother's warmth and visualize her in the kitchen seventeen years later as if it was yesterday. I miss Dad's sense of humour, his knack of making things right. I miss being a daughter. He served his country and by the grace of God came home to make a difference. There is no greater epitaph.

THREE DOZEN MINCE PIES

How is it possible to be shopping for mince pies one minute and entering the glorious gates of Heaven the next? It took a dark and horrible moment in time for the Christmas Fair to be over before it had even begun. My grandmother, Philomena, or Ninnie as she was called, was independent and proud. She was within three months of her 94th birthday.

My mum, her eldest daughter, had died in her sleep twelve years previously. I think they called it "peaceful", but there was nothing peaceful about the shock on my father's face when he woke up and she didn't. A "happy" death reserved for saints, and I can live with the saint bit. It's hard to live without her, even now.

On a Friday morning before the Feast of the Immaculate Conception, Ninnie got up, made the bed and got her purse ready. She locked the door after putting the central heating on. It was a tragic accident. A split second of hell when a frosted window clouded a driver's vision. The coldest day of the year so far. One of those early mornings, 7.20 a.m., that catches your breath and makes your ears go red. We would have talked about the weather, my grandmother and I. Had I seen her, we would have shared that long-winded conversation about the temperature. She worried about falling and breaking a leg.

Ninnie didn't know that it takes at least fifteen minutes to clear a frosted window.

We often spoke about the benefits of central heating and the children of Bosnia. We were next door neighbours for two and a half years. And in between banalities we spoke about how good God was. She adored Our Blessed Lady.

Had her body not been shattered into a thousand pieces, Ninnie would have asked the driver if he was alright. Ordering me to make him a cup of tea with two sugars for shock. The cure for all ills. A cuppa with two sugars for shock. The thousand broken pieces had been through two world wars, and seven home births.

She lay still, the blood red against the snow white of her matted hair. You could smell the cold. You could hold the air. You could even touch eternity. You could sense the shattered hearts that gathered to look.

Had she not been shattered into a thousand pieces, Ninnie would have apologised to Father Jones for getting him up so early. She would have panicked about me being without shoes on a frosty day and Anne, my twin, having to look after three children on her own while her husband was working away. He came home early that week because God knew that Anne needed him.

Ninnie lay staring. She squeezed Anne's hand hard enough to hurt Anne's wedding ring finger. For a while, Ninnie's blood was Anne's. It was an honour and a privilege to share the Last Rites with her, but how can something to shockingly awful be a privilege? I'm not sure, but we met Our Lord and all the angels and saints on that road with Ninnie. I am certain of that. In spite of the horror and the trauma, God's torch shone. I pressed my Rosary to shield her body and the duvet that kept me warm the night before covered the thousand broken pieces that morning. Irene, our cousin's wife, ran screaming to my door and had the presence of mind to get a blanket. I phoned for an ambulance and for Father Jones. I crashed to the ground to be near her. I consoled her and spoke calmly, assuring her that everything would be alright. Glad to be there for her, but not like this. God no, not like this. Her eyes were open and glazed. Staring into the space that had been hers for almost ninety-four years. And all for this.

"You'll be alright now, Nain, we're getting help," I whispered. How can you mend a thousand pieces? I know that she heard a calm voice in the horror. She squeezed Anne's hand. She knew we were there and that meant everything to us.

People rose from their breakfast tables and the crowd came. As they do when there is something to see. Ninnie was clothed in the love of God. We were witnessing a Crucifixion. Ninnie was experiencing the Crucifixion. It was dark and dreadful. It wasn't fair. And everyone looked on.

The duvet was warm. We consoled ourselves with the thought of blanket security for a small child. She looked like a small child under the patterned quilt. Snug as a bug in a rug. But so shattered. And so broken.

The ambulance took her away to cries of "Why couldn't she go in her sleep?" and "Where is her God?" I couldn't speak, for there was nothing to say. I collected her milk. I thought she'd be in hospital for a while. Why couldn't she have slept in that morning? It wouldn't have mattered then if his windows were frozen over. Why didn't you wait for me to get the mince pies? I offered to. But she was so independent, and that was her right. A few minutes' difference and he wouldn't have robbed you of the Queen's telegram. One stupid act destroyed a lifetime of faith and wisdom. How can something so shatteringly secular be so holy? So Catholic? This was her moment in Christ. The Paschal Mystery, Anne called it. The walking out into Jerusalem, the Gethsemane in the middle of the road and the Crucifixion. Her peacefulness was the Resurrection. Her leap into Heaven was the Resurrection. She met the living God that morning. It was her finest hour. But it didn't feel that way. It felt like Hell. And what did she think of before he hit her? I pray that it happened so fast that she didn't have time to think at all. That blink of an eye. That's all it took. And if she was frightened, I know that Our Lord was with her and Our Blessed Mother.

Someone said, "She's given her life to God, it's not fair". If there was ever a moment to bear witness, this was it. But I said nothing. Words were so empty. Shock set in. That sense of unreality that makes you think that you are acting in a movie. And you will wake up and it won't have happened.

Lord, did you look away for a second? Did you forget how old she was? Did you not know that the car windows were frozen solid? God, why didn't you stop the car? Couldn't you have given him a flat tyre? She was buying mince pies for the Fair to honour Your Blessed Mother; where were you when she needed you?

I cringed at my lamentations. Me, I've got lots of faith but I can't help myself. She loved you, God, more than anyone I know. Were you not looking? Silence. Only silence.

Lord, I agreed with the ones that don't know who you are. She didn't deserve this, but I should know better because I love you. I know who you are. They don't. Forgive me. Forgive her if there was anything left unconfessed. You shouldn't have done this, God, and left us cold on the pavement. Not like this. Ninnie, your servant. The little old lady with enough faith for all of us. She was glad we practised the Faith. Molly's girls.

I washed the quilt cover and drank tea. We heard just before ten o'clock that she had died on the way to hospital, thirty miles away.

Anne and David were at the 10 o'clock Mass. Claire had phoned the convent for prayers and I cried in disbelief. Everyone gathered together. It seemed important to be dignified and Catholic. It's what she would have wanted. But it was hard.

The Christmas tree was ready and the children were excited. David picked the kids up and told them the sad news, in case they heard it on the way home from strangers. I explained to Rebecca what had happened as honestly as I could.

Going around my head was, Lord, not this way. Not like this. Not by another man's hand. I blame you enough to ask you why you didn't stop him. Nothing is impossible to you. We know that and we love what that means, but there is no sense here. She was defenceless and frail. You knew that. And the car still threw her up in the air, like a rag doll.

I'm not holy or gracious, but neither were the actions of this lad. Why should I be plagued with guilt at these unkind thoughts? Let me have my tantrums and I'll get back to you, God, when I am less emotional and shocked. They say she's in Heaven and I don't need them to tell me. I *know* she's in Heaven. I just don't like how she got there. I am human too. It's nearly Christmas and we feel as if the car has hit us too. It might as well have, shattered families doing ridiculous but necessary things.

Carrying on because she would have wanted that. Her

generation doesn't ask why, and we are post-Vatican II so we are allowed. Don't ask me to deny the horror and the shock and the cold. Don't ask me to be rational and holy when the same bloody quilt covers me up at night. I have feelings too. I would have taken that knock instead of her. She was so small she didn't stand a chance. I would have been young enough and big enough. The pompous, righteous ones want us to put it behind us. After all, she was old but, God, I can't bear the images of brokenness and the despair of not being able to do something. I kept her warm and I prayed with the priest. If I knew that she wasn't going to make it I would have carried her in my arms and taken her home.

The ones who told us to forgive didn't see her shattered body on that frozen road. They have no right to patronise, God; what happened to love and compassion? Why can't they understand how much it hurts? Why can't they comprehend the horror of a car accident and the brutality involved? I expect it's easier to utter nonsense and then walk away. But what about those who are left, Lord, what about us?

WATCHING YOU WATCHING NOTHING

His tortured eyes roam the hospital side room. What can you see? A light, perhaps? Shadows of a past diminished by dementia. This is my father's brother. He is as helpless as a newborn baby. But he does not know it. He fought for King and country and he stares. Do you remember anything?

I hold his hand. A firm grip for a frail body. "Yes, I'm here; do you remember Jane, Will's girl?" Anne's here too, she's the sensible one, takes after your side of the clan.

I do so want you to know that we are here. Sitting right next to you. The cot sides are covered in some green rubber stuff. I struggle to reach your hand. How did you get here, my friend?

Anne says that she feels God's peace when she sits with you. A sacredness that the secular world cannot, or does not want to, possess. To the world you have lost your usefulness. Too old and dependent. I hate the world too. I'd rather sit with you and God. He is here too. Others may not see him.

I wish you wouldn't stare into nothingness. I wish you would say something. You squeeze my hand. You are speaking, but it's not our language. It makes no difference.

Tell me that you feel alright about being in this state. This condition is acceptable to you. You did not wish it, no-one did. This is you, uncle, and everyone is here. Watching you watching nothing. And it's so disturbing to bear witness to such helplessness.

I've seen a stroke, cancer, road accident – this is different. It has no beginning or end. This staring into space is killing everyone except you.

We analyse in our "let's outwit God" mode and find no answers. As usual. We want Him to take you home so that we don't have to watch you. How dare we!

I've even cursed the euthanasia lot, yet I know in my heart that the Moment of Death belongs only to the one who owns it. People must not be killed because they unnerve us.

I talk to you about our Christmas preparations, the old days in the Black Lion, and the weather. You are making me search my soul in a new way. I'm not sure what will be revealed. You are telling the world, "I am here, I can't lift a cup to my mouth or brush my hair but you have to watch me. I demand it. I'm not going anywhere because I can't. I may have lost my faculties but I am a human being."

OK God, you are. That's why we are here. We have come not out of duty or false piety. We have come to "stay with you awhile".

If this isn't Gethsemane, I don't know what is. It is sacramental. It is beautiful but it brings tears to our eyes. It's a privilege to give you a drink. To wipe your lips. To reassemble the ruffled pyjamas. It's more than "doing". It is partaking in something so touching. You drink and stare and drink some more. You are that war hero. The same person. Your dignity is what draws us here. Any sane person would shut off and make excuses. I have done so in the past. Not anymore. This is your agony and you must not, will not, bear it alone.

I sing Vera Lynn songs. Anne tells me to be quiet. "He wants to sleep," she says. She is right. I need him to hear

"White Cliffs of Dover". He needs nothing except our presence. Maybe not even that. It makes us feel better. Why? Because no-one should live here, staring into nothingness without a hand to hold. No-one should endure this humiliation alone. God said so.

This is the heart of Christianity. What He spoke of in the Gospels. This is your brother and mine. Don't look away, don't you dare call yourself a Christian and ignore those empty eyes. Don't say you can't cope, because he has to. His closest family have to. We are his nieces and it's hurting us. Don't walk around your cosy world, pontificating about loving, and ignore this man's family. The thousands like him in EMI units.

It's not pleasant to witness. This is his Cross. If you look away you are not who you say you are. If catheters and false teeth in a jar make you cringe, then tough. This could be you or me. If the frustration in not being able to communicate is strangling you, then show some empathy towards his children. They have watched this for years.

He is not well at all. It's no good saying you don't like hospitals. No-one does. He needs you. His family needs you. Those empty eyes need you. They are Christ's eyes looking down from the Cross.

I read him my aunty's Christmas card. It's his gift from her. He has a right to hear the lovely words. The greeting. The love. He may not understand, but he has the right to hear.

Are you lonely? Does your conscious mind allow you to understand what you have lost? No-one knows. Not even the experts. Don't feel alone, we're here. I wish we could stay here longer. There's a family at home and washing to sort out.

Do you feel the parting, when we say "Goodnight, God Bless"? Please say you're not scared. I couldn't stand that. You are okay, aren't you? You feel the warm hands and soft words. Something must connect. It does not really matter. We are here. We are still here filling that emptiness, if only for a second.

Some talk to you as if you were a small child. So patronising. They must have a real fear of something in their lives. You are an adult and you deserve the right to be spoken to as an adult. You are that veteran who came back from Burma. These nurses and these visitors, you and I, would not walk in freedom if it were not for those such as my dad and my brave uncle. This would kill my father. I'm glad he died suddenly. This lingering business is awful. It's big, it's black and it feels like someone covering your mouth. This is his reality. We must enter into it or die.

"See you tomorrow," and the next day is just the same. Pretending to be useful. Hoping he hears us as much for our sake as his. And nothing has changed. Only the pyjamas and the bed linen. I want to be here and I don't know why. Does it matter?

I place my Rosary in his hand. I need to bless him. Anne says I talk too much. She's right. I like to sing him to sleep. We argue over opening the window. I want to bring a piece of the outside into this Hell. Anne says he'll catch a draught. We compromise, tell him about our disagreement and the lump in the throat tightens.

Oh God, is this what your son bled for? What purpose does this wretchedness serve? It makes me nervy and edgy, but it makes my heart burst with compassion. Anne has wondered too. There is a sacramental element here.

The sharing of a peace that can't be found "out there".

Where unpleasant smells are abhorrent. Where anything less than perfect just will not do.

There is an honesty and a brutality in this room. There is nowhere to run. There is no need to run. Just "stay awhile", sitting, holding hands, whispering endearments. Hoping against hope that God's love touches his brow as we kiss him goodnight. This patient is not a dementia sufferer, he is my uncle. He has a name. Remember that.

CHRONIC ILLNESS

I make some tea and sit in bed. Obstacle number three is looming. Washing up the milk-soaked pan. Switching the gas off. The Fairy Liquid falls into the washing-up bowl. Bubbles fly. I can't even do this properly. Oh well, everything is clean. The milk pan is kept safely under the sink. My back muscles scream and it's only a small job. I hang up the handtowels. Have a quick look around. It will have to be good enough. Becuase I can't do anymore. It's not my will. It's not like me to ignore cleaning jobs. But that me has gone.

I'm hurting from the inside out. A simple job. Hot chocolate for Rebecca and a friend who's just lost her grandmother. Nurture them. Show them compassion with sugar in the chocolate. I check that they are settled in bed. In their new dressing gowns. Is it only two weeks since Christmas?

The girls are laughing. I yell, "Goodnight. There's school tomorrow." They have enjoyed the hot chocolate.

And nothing changes. I don't have enough muscle power to nurture. To love.

Wow, Jane, think positive. You have performed a valuable task! Get out of bed and open the fridge. Obstacle number one. My back aches, in that deep way, as I crouch to get the milk bottle. We always have too much milk. I don't have the heart to cancel the milkman, who is regular and loyal and needs the money.

Then I stretch to switch the hob on. Obstacle number two. My right arm feels as if it's being stretched to its limits. On a rack of pain like the martyrs. God, I'm only switching the gas hob on.

I manage to open the hot chocolate without exhausting myself. One, two, three scoops. Two sugars. Her grandmother's just died. She needs that feeling of being understood. Without words. Without fuss.

Me, I sit here watching the news on TV. I'm lonely. This one's too big. For Paul. For Anne. For anyone. Helplesness washes over me. Like a baby faltering. It was only a small task. A normal, small, minute part of the day. Only it's not normal at all. Paul says I've lost my sense of humour. I tell him to get lost.

What have you achieved today, Jane? I've made two cups of hot chocolate. Washed up. Got angry. Well done. Think of the love you have demonstrated. Think of the laughter and the children. We all get tired, Jane. We're not getting any younger. You need extra vitamins, that's all.

Leave me alone. Get lost. I know you will never understand what this is doing to me. For I would not understand if it were you. So go away. I'd rather hurt on my own. Where no-one can see me trying and failing and dying that little bit more. Every time I don't manage to perform a simple task.

Jean Vanier said:

> Compassion is a word full of meaning. It means sharing the same passion, sharing the same suffering, sharing the same agony, accepting into my heart the misery in yours. Your pain calls out to me. It touches my heart. It awakens something within me, and I become one with you in your pain. I may not be able to relieve your pain,

but by understanding it, sharing it, I make it possible for you to bear it, in a way that enhances your dignity, and helps you to grow.

Please understand that I don't want you to do anything. Don't feel sorry for me because I am alright. I will be alright. So long as I don't look too far ahead. Don't leave me wishing that I was different. I am me. I can't be different. This is who I am.

Hold out your hand to me. Make tea if you have a mind to. Tell me about your day. I am interested. I want to know what's going on out there in the world of movement. Where feet move fast and furious. What does it feel like to walk properly? To stand tall and straight and pretty. I suppose it's a bit like breathing. It's automatic. Do you have to be "different" to feel self-conscious? No. Even models have hang-ups. Open any newspaper and feel the emptiness of the perfect people. Walking isn't a panacea for lasting fulfilment. My conscious mind tells me that but I can't help feeling that it gives you a head start. Not being physically disabled, I mean. The "if only's" are more poignant because the options are so few.

I'm fine, really I am. What do I want? Your hand in mine. Your laughter and gaiety. Bad moods and the occasional crisis. Be you so that I can be me. So that we can share a moment. Cherish a minute or an hour. Open your heart and be true to yourself. So that we can be real in our exchanges. Discard your defences and come to me naked and vulnerable. For this is what my life is. Exposed and raw. Feeling every hurt deeply, mentally but mostly physically. But I am open and true. My brick wall has been eroded by events. I have had to sit "in it". In the mire and the shadows. Don't be afraid of just "being".

If you remain with me long enough, I will help you endure your powerlessness. I will "watch with you". Listen until you are done with soliloquising. I will empathise and walk your walk. Jump into your skin, if I have to. I can feel what you feel. What do I want from you? The same acceptance and love that I offer you freely. No strings or conditions. No agenda. If you really want to assist me in this difficult journey, just love me. And then I may, just may, be able to bear it.

Sadly, few are able to empathise with me in the way that I need them to. To a certain extent, I blame myself for their inadequacies. I must be giving out the wrong signals. How can you say I'm your friend and yet you fail to understand the real essence of my being?

Perhaps I don't look different enough. Can't you see my misshapen hands and wasted muscles? Look at my elbows and tell me that I am normal. See my skin, as thin as paper after years of steroids. This is why my weight goes up and down, and you still talk about diets and aerobics as if they have any part of my life. Have you not understood?

Or is it that you think I could walk further if I tried hard enough? If I pushed past that pain barrier and exercised more mind over matter?

Perhaps I shouldn't have taken those tablets over twenty years ago. Is that what you think? Don't you know that I had no control? Permission was never granted and doctors knew best. Those pompous men with their arrogant walk and probing eyes. If I was your child, would you have done to them what you did to me? I doubt it.

Why does it have to be anyone's fault? When you look at me, are you worried that this could be you in twenty years' time? If you share some tea with me, are you wary of catching something? The guessing is insane. All you have to be is honest. Do I upset you? Do I remind you of your grandmother? I don't mind. Please tell me what you think, for silence just exacerbates my isolation.

WHY DOES MY VULNERABILITY SCARE YOU SO?

When you look at me, do I disconcert you? Are you afraid of catching these dreadful conditions that I suffer from?

I'm weary, tired of struggling hopelessly against the tide. I want permission to tell you this, otherwise I cannot be real.

Why can't I tell you that I am frightened? You are my friend. Is this too much to ask?

I talk to God. He accepts me as I am. He sees me whole. He sees me scared. God, the Invisible, Omnipotent One. He does not judge or make assumptions. So what gives you the right to do so?

I need to cry but tears go unshed. I need to release my pain. To rage, scream and shout. Solutions are useless. They may well make you feel better but they do nothing for me. So you need protecting. You need your feelings spared. Because you will not let me own my being.

Can't you see dark circles under my eyes? See the tremor in my hands? Why does my pain frighten you? I'm not asking you to take it from me. I'm pleading with you to bear it with me.

Jesus walks with me. He is in me. I am in Him. This is my Truth. My gift from the Lord of Compassion. He chose me to be this way for a purpose. He made me vulnerable. Powerless.

To be vulnerable is to be wounded. To stay with that

despair until it strangles you. To want to say "yes", when your screams say "no". To cry out in pain and hear nothing.

The dark night is a bottomless pit. An abyss of a terrifying tomorrow. A sea of doubt and disappointment. A dying of wants and desires. A surrender of will. With a deep disappointment that my will is not God's.

So you go to Mass. Do you realise how much God suffered for His Son's humanity? That walk to Golgotha. The agony in the Garden. I bet you're glad you have had a charmed existence. You cannot be real if you don't feel Jesus's fear. His anguish. He broke the bread. Offered His body as a sacrifice for your doubts. The covenant of love was given to us. A last goodbye or an au revoir? The gift of His Body and Blood. To strengthen and give courage.

The Last Supper made things right with the Father. Don't eat it and assume holiness. You must live and breathe the Spirit. Take it and eat it. It is the body and blood of the Lamb. No man in history has given so freely for so many. Underestimate the love and you have not listened to a word.

If you fail to grasp the meaning of love, then you will not understand Christ's Gethsemane. If you wince when you hear the Passion, you will never face your own vulnerability. This means that you will miss the very reason for living. To be scared, anxious, full of defences – this is not life. This is Hell.

If you are in pain, you are in the Garden with Jesus. Oh, but how can we possibly compare our suffering to His? Easily. He became human to be one of us. Not to make us inadequate and inept. He became human to hurt like us. To feel the fear and disappointments like us. Why would God bother to send His only Son if it wasn't to enhance our understanding? The entire purpose was to make us love more.

> This is my body, this is for you; do this in a memorial of me. This cup is a new covenant in my blood. Wherever you drink it, do this as a memorial of me. (St. Paul/Cor. 11: 23–26)

Gethsemane is our human condition. We have all been hurt, although many deny this. Denial is useful. Denial eradicates guilt, resentment and terror. It blocks off feelings.

Denial is manifested in many forms. I used to clean all the time. If my house was clean and in order, then my life would be also. People would believe that if my house was clean, then I was in control. Cleaning gives one a routine, a feeling of being cleansed and understood. I was not cleaning out of wanting to be clean and tidy. I was cleaning because I was very unhappy.

You can't say that you are unhappy, so you carry on – the house gets shinier whilst inside the turmoil bubbles. To sit down is to experience that turmoil. To clean is to send it packing until the next pause for thought.

To pause for a moment is to feel vulnerable and, for some ludicrous reason, being vulnerable disturbs us greatly.

Vulnerability is not a state which, once you come out of, goes away. It is an essential part of humanity. We can grapple with it. Play around. Pretend we are not and, even if we are vulnerable, so what?

Jesus Christ's vulnerability reached a crescendo in the agony of the Garden.

"Stay here while I go over to pray" (Matthew 26: 14–27–66). He needed company. He needs to know that His friends are close by. He needs to know love. Jesus prays.

Here is a man, divine and human, praying at that very moment He needs God the most.

Jesus prays. His friends. Those disciples. He has lived with and loved for so long cannot see that the Master is "cracking up". Are they blind? Does it hurt them to realise that Jesus is in grave danger? Of course it does, so why can't they "stay awhile"?

They may fear for their own safety. They may be in awe after the breaking of the bread. There is a possibility that they were quite simply exhausted.

Whatever the reasons, His mates let him down big time.

We have all been there. Promised ourselves that we will not let it happen again. Our pride is hurt and many friendships are ruined because one or the other was not big enough to say, "I'm sorry". Too stubborn to forgive.

So there it is. The Son of Man, crushed by the burden of humanity. The Omnipotent One, on His knees, praying to His Father to "let this cup pass me by". (Matthew 26: 14–27–66).

"Sorrowful to the point of death." His heart was broken. No pride here. No place for rationale and logic.

He was on His knees. Today, it would be called a nervous breakdown. Collapse. Can't take any more.

GETHSEMANE

I'll stay awake, my Lord, until midnight at least. But I cannot sit still. Cannot pray. Thoughts invade that which should be empty. Tonight of all nights. When You need me, us, why is it impossible to come up with the goods? I'm awake, I'm thinking of You. Is this enough?

Why are human beings so selfish and limited? Sure, we have martyrs and heroes, but they are an exception. Most of us are scared and restless and confused. Is this You in the Garden of Olives?

Disappointed and agitated. Aggrieved at the lack of human warmth. Aghast at the betrayal of Judas. Your life in exchange for a few pieces of silver? You are worth more than that. That's why Judas hanged himself.

But are we not just as guilty? Of not keeping Your name. Of running with the mob because it's not the done thing to be a Christian. Our children go to Mass and that isn't cool. They go because we tell them to, until they are old enough to grasp the enormity of Your gift to them.

Aren't You angry? For the miracles and the good deeds must seem distant tonight. They took what they wanted and ran away. They drained Your compassionate heart and let it bleed. They watched Your mother at the foot of the Cross. A mother of all mothers.

Did You weep out of fear or out of disappointment? Your mates fell asleep. Some mates, eh? Were You anticipating the nails in the thud of the wooden cross? You are the son of God. You're not supposed to be scared. You are Omnipotent. But You were scared, weren't You?

You collapsed at the Father's feet and wept. How can we compare our sorrow to Yours? That deeply-felt pit where the soul lives. That place that hurts because someone has not loved enough. Someone has not believed that we mattered enough. This is the ultimate sin. Omission.

A priest once said that we are either in the Garden with You, or on the fence. I used to believe in this all-or-nothing philosophy. That we were faithful and true and nothing less.

I wish! We are human. We try and we fail. We are limited and egotistical and childish. We are proud. You are the perfect human being. You knew all of this and You loved anyway. You knew that free will would win, and still You bled to death for our sins.

Gethsemane is home to most of us. In one way or another. It may be mental anguish or physical distress. Doubt and fear. Gethsemane is the wounded spirit. The lost soul. The bleeding heart. The bereaved and lonely.

Tonight, Holy Thursday, is about coping with all of this. You uttered "Thy will be done", from the depths of Your heart. You screamed for Your God and You were transformed. Became strong. Took up Your Cross. Thank You for this. For the example of all examples.

No running away for You. No denial and quick getaway. Lame excuses. You took of the cup, ate it and drank it. We are meant to do the same.

I eat and drink from Your cup too. But I am still scared and alone. Not always, of course. There are many blessings, but there is a separation from You that I find destroyingly painful. I cannot be perfect. In faith and trust I endeavour and fail. I give to one person and neglect the others.

I cannot be in two places at one time. I cannot love two people with the same love. I can't tolerate those I should. I can't be placid and serene. But when I say I love You I should be all these things. At least some of the time.

I demand authenticity in all aspects of my life. It doesn't happen. Why? Because everyone is too busy or too afraid or both. Those who do not practice the faith are often kinder to me that those who do. They demonstrate acts of love that are saintly. And yet they may never grace a church door.

I'll tell You what really bugs me – it's the ones who say the Lord's Prayer and don't even ask or care if I live or die. My pain means nothing to them. Just a nuisance. I'm not useful practically, therefore I do not count.

Your friends knew You well. They ate with You. They witnessed the miracles and heard the parables and still they ran a mile when the going got tough. So what hope do I have? Or any of us?

I'm often accused of being too open. Emotionally and verbally. To me there is no other way to be. I make myself vulnerable, they say. So what! We are all vulnerable but we are darned if we let on.

I am open because I've got nothing to hide. I know my imperfections, my fears and anxieties. I also know my strengths. Whatever these are, they are gifts from God. Even pride and ego.

The subconscious mind is very clever. It hides the imperfections but, sooner or later, the conscious mind wakes up. It has to face the beast. That ugliness and feebleness. All those things that we try to mask with drink, drugs or whatever. We push this subconscious awareness away until the next time.

Only the next time comes closer and closer until one day we wake up and cannot ignore the dark side of ourselves. You can tell it to go away. It makes no difference. It might make our addictions worse and one day it will literally kill us. This fear. This anger. This Beast within!

You said "Thy Will be done" and meant it. We say it, I say it, and want to believe that I mean it but in my heart of hearts I, we, don't. Why not? Because I am not as brave as You. We want to follow You as long as it doesn't cost too much. As long as it doesn't hurt too much.

"Thy will be done," as long as You do it my way. What hypocrisy! And You died for this. When things are rosy it's easy to chat parrot-fashion, then crawl when things go wrong. When illness strikes and dares to interrupt our plans. Why me? Why them? Why not? You died to share in our suffering. You never guaranteed three score years and ten. You guaranteed love. A love that would carry us through and beyond. Gethsemane.

You guaranteed forgiveness, no matter what we do. This was not meant as a licence to kill, but You suffered it as a gift. A grace. How we throw it back in Your face!

It's Good Friday today. What did You see as You gazed through blood-filled eyes? Your Mother, destroyed and dying from grief. John, Your faithful favourite. Your fellow prisoners. You promised the Good Thief a place in Heaven. In Your pain You answered not only absolution but forgiveness for the repentant sinner. The death-bed confessor. You put aside the horror of Your dying in order to console a common thief. Why? Because You believe that love and compassion and mercy comes before all else. Even Your own death. This man needed Your grace. He didn't have to bother. He was dying too. But He knew that You were God.

As for the other thief, what arrogance! A sheer blatant disregard for his wrongdoings. No concern for Judgement Day here. These two had a choice. One chose eternal life, the other chose death. Why did the one have faith and other nothing but defiance?

Did You see your friends, or were they hiding? Fearing for their lives. Sitting on the fence because to know You would mean the same grisly fate. And Peter, crushed by his denial, grasping at anything that would make everything alright. You saw the guards and the spectators. Did You feel betrayed, or had that been dispelled in the Garden? I hope that You saw the love around You. Veronica's compassion, and Simon of Cyrene's too. They loved You even if they killed You.

What do You see today, my Lord? Repentant sinners going to Mass. Believing that You died and rose again. Celebrating the great victory over death. The unrepentant thieves ignore the day and fly abroad or do some do-it-yourself. Totally disregarding the greatest event in history. This makes me sad. And angry too. But what do You see? The potential for change and redemption for the non-believers. We have the gift of faith, but we abuse it. It's our job to love the unrepentant thieves and show them Your face.

I don't try to convert anymore. It's too exhausting and it's not my job. I once naïvely and foolishly thought I could change people's beliefs. I can't.

I can only hope that, by worshipping You from a wheelchair, one person in my lifetime just may think that there is something in this God business. I believe because of the despair and the powerlessness and the hopelessness. I believe in spite of it all. This is my message. Thank You for the Cross. For dying for a sinner like me. For showing me how to endure and offering me the grace of acceptance. I bowed to the Cross today. I'm proud to be Your servant. I have a long way to go. Without sacramental eyes I would have been destroyed. With Your love, I am here. Unworthy but faithful.

THE MEANING OF SUFFERING

Suffering is very noble as long as it's not yours. It is an honourable thing to own. It is what saints do best. Oh, yes, it is holy and Christ-like as long as it is not happening to you. Carrying the Cross is great as long as you don't have to do it. As long as it's not your tears making the pillowcase damp. Being Catholic and ill is doubly burdensome because you feel obliged to be glad. Compelled to accept your suffering because you are sharing in Our Lords's Passion. You want to share the pain but without the suffering. You want to help Jesus Christ on His way to Calvary. But only for a little while; life would be fair if everyone lifted the weight off His shoulders. It's not like that, though. Why? I don't want to "fight the good fight" although I suspect I will have to. I want to be alright. I want easy movement and flights of fancy. God, I did not choose this illness but You did. I know You did, but I thought you loved me. Why, then? Why me, when anyone else would have done? Since it is Your will and not mine you could have at least made me holy. Remotely holy. I have often wished that You hadn't bothered. Forgive these bitter moments, but I am only human. You can't have got it right, Lord. Your silence is torturing me. Where are my joyous ecstasies, Lord? The dazzling bright lights? No vision, but I know that You are there. Even if You won't talk to me. I have always believed in You. To be weak is to be strong. Not in this secular world it isn't. To be weak is to be weak.

Lord of compassion, why don't You hear me? I loathe the emptiness that You are meant to fill. Where is the peace You spoke about? Why do You hurt me when all I do is love You? There can be no glory in pain; if there was, I would have found it. There can be no glory in not being able to cuddle your child! And You speak of love. I can't brush my little girl's hair and You expect me to accept. Forgive me if I can't. Forgive me if I won't. How do You think that I feel when I know that this is Your doing? I was born for this. Before I was even conceived this is what was prepared for me. You knew that the laughter would go, replaced by a crippling illness. When I did my First Holy Communion, I was so proud. A Bride of Christ. So why then destroy my childhood? I went to Catechism classes and Holy Mass every Sunday. Couldn't You alter the plan when You discovered that I was a good girl? Or was it too late and You couldn't go back? Couldn't You change your mind and give the sickness to someone who didn't go to Mass? Someone who didn't think that there was a God? Why my family? Lovely, decent people. You knew that I had a mother who was ill. What about her, Lord? Didn't you care about her? What made You think that we could bear it? Did you know something that we didn't? Is that why You gave us Faith? Did you think that it would be enough?

It was, at times, but You weren't around when we needed You. And You haven't answered all the prayers. You haven't always been there and sometimes you were very quiet. You didn't let on. I could have stopped loving You years ago when You took Josie away from me.

I could have looked away and never come back. I wanted her more than You. I was her mother. And I still gave you glory, even thanking you for allowing her to fall asleep with dignity. But still You will not take this pain from me.

Sure, suffering is honourable as long as your child doesn't die before you. Before she can play on the swings and watch *101 Dalmatians*. Tell those people in your churches that they are supposed to love You through it. Show them how hard life can be and stop picking on someone who tries.

I'm not particularly proud of my protestations, but You know what is in my heart so there is no point in being hypocritical. You hate that more than anything. You don't like pretence and camouflaging; this is me and I am tired and ungracious. You know that because You understand suffering. You, Lord, know what it's like. This is why I find no relief so hurtful because I love You and I know that You can help me. So I get upset when You don't. What I find strange is that even though I have been angry with You, I have never doubted that You are God. Anguished rages and squealing tantrums, but I've never denied You. You know that. And I could have turned away. So many, many times. Your Love tortures me. It grips my soul with gentle arms and still nothing changes.

Oh yes, I've kept Your name. I've said "God is good" with my heart breaking. You must know the pain, watching the world destroy itself. What must you feel when You see the hunger and the killing? Do you cope because You are Jesus Christ? Does Your divinity protect You? I hope so. Does Your compassion fuel Your aching heart? Why don't You do something?

I'm sorry You laid down Your life. No-one can do more than that. Were we worth it? Would You do it again, or would You think twice? I wouldn't die for murderers and raving megalomaniacs. For the greedy and unscrupulous.

But You did. You love them as much as You love me, and yet You spare them. You allow them too walk around without pain to violate and blaspheme. I wouldn't hurt a fly!

You have a special place in Your heart for the sick. So why don't You step in when the suffering destroys? Do You send somebody else? Someone kind and thoughtful to cushion the blows? A living Christ disguised in the sympathetic nurse and the compassionate neighbour? Someone with a light in them? A light that glows in terrible darkness.

How can I help others when I am sick? I would go shopping for the housebound and comfort those in pain. I could love more if I was well. You know my frustration. It's like a warm heart resting in a body made of concrete. Too stiff to move. Too crippled to do Your work on earth. I would be something if You would just say the word. I know I could.

And I have begged You to make me well. I have squirmed and prostrated myself before You in a desolate wretchedness of pain and shocking despair that almost very nearly destroyed my inner soul, and still silence. The void that cannot be filled until I know Your peace. That emptiness that is in the dark. That blackest of holes. Gaping and awful.

I'm glad I came from You, but I don't feel blessed or special. I hate people liking me because I was only ten when I became ill. That is empty. It means nothing. Keep the pity for those who truly deserve it. Like the tragedy of Africa – innocents starving because we have too much. Barren fields because of man's obsession with having it all.

If suffering is to count for something, then good must emerge. If it falls on dead ground then what has it all been about? This great theatre of life. What then, Lord, am I doing here?

What is pain worth? Cumbersome memories for my loved ones to carry, knowing that I was never really free. Reminders of hospitals and failed medical science. The youngest around here to have joint replacement operations. And to have babies afterwards. Surely I am worth more than a passing conversation in the local Post Office, and an intriguing X-ray in a file? I am worth more than my cupboard full of tablets. I am Your child and that matters to me, so why can't You spare me? You spare others, so why not me?

My suffering must not be wasted. That would be unthinkable. I know about eternal joy but I am talking about now. And tomorrow and next week. God, how am I going to live this life in peace? I can't go back to a blind faith. I have to ask. I must know You as my Friend. I need You as a Consoler, not just as a picture to be scared of. Comfort me with a genuinness that I can embrace. Console me with a love that uplifts, not demands. Give me solace. So that I may be filled with the Spirit of belonging. Blanket me with a consolation that bathes the piece of me that has been broken. Because it is Yours to mend. Bring the pieces together, Lord.

I am convinced that the reason I don't recover is because I refuse to accept Your Will for me. We don't quite see eye to eye. I honestly can't see why You would want this for me. Would not any human being who is not perfect want to be free of physical pain? I don't think that I am unreasonable. Ungracious and petulant, perhaps. But not unreasonable. This is not bringing out the best in me, no matter what Your clergy say. They have no right to judge me and to preach when they do not understand the misery that is my being. How dare the? How dare a priest tell me that I should be content with not climbing mountains? I don't want to climb a mountain. That is not the issue. I could see You from a mountain-top. I could smell and even touch You from higher up. I could be near You but You never gave me a chance. I was just ten years old. I could have been a nun or a missionary. I could have given You a life of service if You wanted me to. But you didn't. You chose the Way of the Cross for me. That makes me feel trapped and guilty and hurt because that's not what I want. The Way of the Cross is too hard for me. I want things to be different. Forgive me. Deep in my heart I understand that what You want is more important than my desires. Because you see the whole picture in all its awfulness and all its beauty.

You've seen me down. You know that place where I go when things are difficult. So how low do I have to go before You pick me up? How many blank faces do I have to stare at before I see You? Don't think that people see me and think of You because they don't care. They're too busy playing God. They don't need You like I do. Not until they get ill or lose someone or both.

Who am I to talk like this to the Son of God? I am ashamed. At least it's confessed. That's something! Though it does not hurt any less to say it. Make me brave like martyrs. Encircle me with the love of the saints who said "yes" to You. Tell me that You haven't forgotten me. Illuminate me. Lift me up. Raise me from my human darkness, so that I can see Your face in the wretchedness. Don't leave when I panic and thrash about because that's when I need you the most. Stay with me.

Do you remember that night in Gethsemane? I thought

You went through that so that we wouldn't have to. How could they do that to You? Of all people, Jesus Christ, the Son of Man. You broke down. You were anxious and scared and You needed someone. But no one came. You couldn' t stand it so You gave in God. But You and God are the same. You know the Father. Did that make you less scared? Were You as scared of dying as we are? Or is it different when You are God? Did it hurt any less because You were God, or did it hurt You more?

I would have stayed with You. I would have held Your hand. Your pain meant something. You saved the world. It was a horrible means to a glorious end. And it only lasted for a short time. Forgive me before I say it, but the suffering did not last a lifetime. This is the hardest thing I have ever written. I don't mean to minimise or take anything away. You are my God. But the agony in the garden was for only one night. My agony in the garden seems to have been forever and probably until the day I see You in Heaven. If I get there, that is. Assuming that I do well, will you tell me why? Will it be unspoken, or will Your love make everything okay? Will the hurt be a memory and so finished with? There are no cripples in Heaven, just love and the mystery of God. And the welcome from the One who knows what you've gone through and will make allowances for that.

Should I choose sickness instead of health, maybe? I don't have enough courage to do that. You should know that. You know everything. This is asking the impossible. I don't have to be rich, but I need my health to look after my family. I need health or my sanity. Or is it okay to lose that too? Leave me with nothing. No props. No lifeline. Except You. Is that where I am going wrong? Do I have to lose everyone and everything so that I can see You? I saw You when my child was dying. I saw You when my parents died. Why can't I see You in sickness? Others are broken too. Why must I accept what most would refuse to? Take this burden of guilt for uttering such thoughts, for being without grace, for being me.

I always thought You wanted me to be true. Here I am! Do you still love me? Am I still worthy? Am I less than I was yesterday? I feel released because I have told You how I feel. As if You were sitting beside me. As if You had walked through the front door and sat down. Have I not shared it in the way that You needed me to? If I trust You, do you wonder why? You never promised us anything in this earthly life. I understand the gospel. I know that you owe me nothing. Not here. Not on earth, so why should I expect to get well? Why should I expect anything if it comes to that? I should be content with Heavenly matters. Thoughts of Heavenly glory should be enough, but it isn't. Because I wanted to be well on earth so that I could work for You. I'm no good to You like this. I can barely look after my family, so how can I look after Your people? Do you mind self-pity, or should I count my blessings? I have never felt as sorry for myself as I have now. It was when I realised that You could help me but didn't that I started to drown. Miracles happen all the time. And you know, I always said that I didn't want to ask for a miracle because You made me like this. I was scared of offending You by refusing suffering. I couldn't bear to tell You that it wasn't fair for fear of being struck down. If I lost You then I would have nothing. And I couldn't bear that. I don't think that such suffering is fair. Not every day.

And the road is long and lonely. It feels as if I'm the only one walking it. It shouldn't be like that. Despair doesn't breed holiness. Not for me anyway. Despair is a black tunnel. Despair is being entombed in your suffering. No air. No open door. No love. Lord, bring me back to wholeness before I go out of my mind. If You won't make me well then put some fire into my soul so that it doesn't matter so much. Send me the Holy Spirit to make me great. Send a slice of Heaven down so that I can taste the glory now. Give me that euphoric glow that transcends human experience and I might be able to bear it. Don't expect me to fight this pain with just crumbs for comfort.

The cruellest blow is when I think I'm getting better and another crisis comes. You know it upsets me. You know how much it hurts. Do You not care? If not about me, about my young daughter. And the strain it puts on my husband and family.

I cling to the Rosary. I adore the Blessed Mother, and I pray for others. For souls too. For my departed family. I feel guilty praying for myself, but I do. I beg you, through tears of real despair, as I am at Your mercy. A genuine cry from the heart. I plead and beg for You to intercede and still it's as if You were sleeping. Or just ignoring me, hoping I'd stop whingeing and go to sleep. Even if You don't hear me I come back to You. To beg again. I search for Your strength. If I could absorb it I could be well for a while. But never fully right. Because You never wanted that for me, did You? Otherwise, You would have stepped in years ago.

So do I offer my suffering to the God who has caused it? Or do I become damned and embittered? Let Satan have his way. Let Satan rub his hands with glee. I am supposed to have faith. Where is my strength? Why aren't You enough, Lord? Why should I be a scapegoat anyway? For whose sins am I atoning? What do you think of your reluctant warrior now? Is it a shock to find out that bravery was forced? Put on for the benefit of others. And You, how could I let You down? You made me in a particular way and I didn't dare question your reasons. They wouldn't have been satisfactory anyway. Because I don't deserve this and I can't bear to believe that You think I do. Deserve sounds like a punishment, which is not what God does. I know that. But oh God, it feels like a constant beating and it hurts like fire eating bones. Where are You when I cry after my baby's finally asleep and I am free to show my pain? I know that You are alive in the holy water I wash my face with. And the Rosary I recite at night when sleep won't come. But what of the pain, God; can't You do something about it? Help me when the morning is no different and it starts all over again.

Come to our rescue then, if not for me but for my little girl. Or does my beautiful eight year old have to pay too? For having me as a mother who loves her more than anything? What is she supposed to learn? Compassion and understanding? Or that life is hard and she might as well get used to it? That her mother is an example to others?

Someone once told me that Rebecca would be a better person because of my suffering. He stopped short of saying that it was the best thing that could have happened to her. Having a cripple for a mum. A perfect role model of Christian suffering.

Never mind about the lost evenings spent in bed together playing with dolls because I can't move. I hope the cuddles and laughter will be remembered more than the tears that are shed in darkness. When there is only You, Lord.

I pray too that she sees You as the whole God. I want her

to follow You because she loves You, not because her mother was ill.

Guard me from a bitter heart, so that she may glimpse the glory, Lord. Throw light on the pain so that we can live in the peace of acceptance. Give us the courage not to shine but to endure patiently and always keep Your name, Jesus Christ most Holy.

WHY DOES GOD ALLOW SUFFERING?

Theologians and clever philosophers, believers and non-believers, have grappled with the big question for centuries. It seems only saints know how to suffer gladly, smiling through their despair and ridiculously asking, no, begging for more pain in order to get closer to the Holy Cross.

Does pain exist because, without it, pleasure would be bland? Beauty would vanish because it was all around. The Fall of man from grace goes some way to explain man's choice in how he decides to live his life. Free will. A dangerous but necessary thing.

Many blame God for all the suffering. His Omnipotence makes Him the scapegoat. He can do anything, so why does pain even exist? Surely, the compassionate healer can prevent earthquakes. Stop the car when the child is about to be thrown in the air. Why doesn't He show His greatness, since nothing is impossible? He rose from the dead. Brought Himself back from death. And so why all the agony in this damned and ugly world?

If God is in charge, why doesn't He do something? He asks us to believe, and history reveals that those who believed the most got the short straw. Those early disciples fired by the Holy Spirit were transformed from scared weak men into giants. Hiding in the Upper Room, terrified of the authorities. They knew they'd let Jesus down. Unable to witness the horrific crucifixion of their friend, they cowered and squirmed as He drowned in His blood. Screaming "Father, forgive them, for they know not what they do".

It seems to me that there is a huge chasm regarding logic in seeing and understanding what you have witnessed and the heart which is prone to doubt, fear, angst and all those silly things that cloud judgment.

They had been there at Caanan. When Lazarus was brought back to life. When Jesus drank with unclean women. They had known Him, like you and I know our families and friends. Were they stupid or just plain scared? Both, probably. Simon Peter, the arrogant fisherman. Chosen to be the Rock. Pledging loyalty at the Last Supper just hours before the cock crowed. They loved Jesus, I'm sure of that, but not enough to die for Him. Not until the Pentecost, that is. When the Spirit came down on them and made them real disciples.

The obvious connection here is the Spirit of God, placed in men's hearts to give courage, patience and strength. Courage enough to brave execution and endure torture in the name of the Master.

It does not make sense that the Jesus they knew who healed people's pain at every opportunity would "allow" so much suffering to go unconsoled. Unrewarded. What's the point of following someone who can't guarantee that you won't get cancer? That your child won't be murdered? What kind of God "allowed" the Holocaust to happen?

Valid questions, but only silence. God does not appear to you and me physically. Yet we believe in a loving Creator. We pray and eat of His Body and still get hurt. In fact, the harder we pray the greater the hurt.

It does not make sense. Good people dying young and others murdering and rotting in prisons. Bereaved parents of murdered children having to imagine the cries and the agony of molested flesh and blood. Couldn't God have distracted that murderer? Struck the paedophile down before he could do his worst?

Is it any wonder that God seems aloof and missing? Have you heard them cry "where's your God now" and been left speechless? Well, there are no answers, but still a deep certainty that He is there. In the most appalling tragedy. He is there. I know that. I have seen it in my own experiences. I don't know why Josie died. I don't understand why my mother had to suffer so much. I can't explain His plans for me because I am not God.

I am a sinner. Unworthy of grace or His love and understanding. I feel Him sometimes. More often than not, He is silent. On the darkest days He does not deserve my loyalty, my witness and my prayers of thanksgiving. What arrogance! I've often wondered why I bother to love Him. It certainly doesn't feel like a two-way relationship. But still I pray. Does that make me a ridiculous optimist? Do I secretly, in that deepest place, believe that one day I will wake up and walk without pain and the struggle will be over?

No. If God had wanted me to have easy mobility, He could have cured me years ago. He deserves my soul, my spirit, my love. My physical state is of no consequence to Him. What comes out of my mouth and my heart most definitely is. How do I know this? I don't know. I just do. No-one has told me directly.

God has spoken to my heart. He has offered me grace and I am truly blessed. I can't throw it back in His face on a really bad day, even if I want to. And I do. Believe me, I'm no martyr. I don't enjoy pain. But I enjoy grace. I experience it when the pieces are falling around me.

As I write this, my body is in a continual painful spasm so why, I ask myself, do I feel blessed? Why don't I put the pen down and read a book? Or just watch the television? Because I need to explain to you that suffering can be borne. No pain or catastrophe can be worse than losing God's favour.

Last week I was told that the last hope for my muscle problem was being suspended. The Botox injections worked the first time. The second and third lot failed. Why did I have false hopes, and then a locked door? I had great relief for seven weeks after six injections. Naturally, I expected the treatment to work. So that I would have less pain for a while at least.

If God knew, and He knows everything, why did I have to endure sixteen more Botox injections when He knew the outcome? Gobowen Hospital is a two-hour journey from home. The injections aren't pleasant, so why the false hope? I don't know. The disappointment went deep but I bounced back. I don't stay depressed too long, thank God.

Of course, I cried and had some private dramatic "Thanks a bunch, God" days, but I know that the professionals, Dr Morgan and Lyn, will help me no matter what. They will not give up on me. God will not give up on me.

Do I blame Him for the failure of the treatment? No. It's not His will. His desire for me is to see the compassion and love in that hospital. To value it, and embrace it. I saw nurses tending broken bones with genuine sympathy. I was given three cups of tea after my treatment. I was treated with kindness and positive regard and, believe me, this is rare.

I know that Dr Morgan has referred me to his colleague because of this mysterious muscle problem. I trust him. That's God's love manifested in individuals who may not even know it. It's there just the same.

Hand on my heart, my physical state stinks. And yet I know that I will be okay.

Brother Loarne Ferguson, a friar at Pantasaph, has been a tremendous source of comfort. He is compassionate, funny and holy. He listens to my whingeing and my wailing and he makes things right between me and God.

I don't need solutions. I need support, both physically and psychologically. More importantly, I need spiritual guidance and Brother Loarne offers it to me. Freely and without conditions. Had the injections worked, I would not have called on Brother Loarne. I would not need the help and care of Mark Carter, the hypnotherapist. He listens to my jokes and tantrums and helps me reduce the muscle pain for an hour at least. I can self-hypnotise if I'm in the right frame of mind.

It's not God who fails me. It's medical science. The more despairing I become, the more I cling to God. To Paul and my sisters and brother. My friends, Father Clarke, my parish priest, Chris my neighbour and our cosy chats.

My place in suffering is small. The earthquake in India is real suffering. Those who have no faith is Hell. I know this. I see the consequences of Godlessness daily. The lack of taking responsibility. This ridiculous search for meaning in a new cooker or new settee. It doesn't work. I try to tell them this and still they refuse to bring down the defences.

Real suffering is rejection by parents. Living in an

unemployment blackspot with only a giro to wait for and mouths to feed. Parents of missing children left wondering for years. Family feuds and petty jealousy. This is despair. This is hopelessness too.

As far as horrendous pain goes, God did not cause the Holocaust. A certain individual did and the crows followed him. People such as Edith Stein, Dietrich Bonhoeffer and Corrie Ten Boom saw God in the concentration camps. Many others could not do it. I don't blame them. I doubt whether I would have been able to see Him if my parents had been gassed and my siblings tortured to death.

Why does suffering make some people great and others fall into a terrible abyss? Why do individuals moan about hideously ridiculous things whilst others rise to the occasion and teach us to grow? The Holy Spirit, God's gift to us. Sacramental eyes and open hearts. I am blessed but not holy. The saints and the martyrs were both. I love God but I couldn't face being eaten by a lion in His defence.

Does that make me a hypocrite? A human being? Do I feel deep down that I have suffered enough? Yes. Honest, but not humble. I'm well aware of my spiritual shortcomings. Could I leave my family and live on an island, just me and God? No. I need people around me. I get anxious without reassurance and company. Am I an authentic disciple, then? I doubt it very much.

At least I know it. I don't masquerade behind holiness pretending to love. Feigning compassion but not getting too close in case it disturbs my equilibrium – I don't chant the Rosary and ignore the suffering at the same time.

I haven't taken the vows to serve God and then defiled them by expecting to be served. Yet is seems that the Church lets the groans of suffering go unconsoled. We don't pray hard enough. We don't try hard enough. I could walk if I really tried to. Mind over matter.

Time and time the believers fail us. And non-believers too. It's more hurtful when church people condemn us to the role of the sick. They read the Gospel. They know what they must do. And yet they run around, judging and condemning the very hearts they should console. I find this more disturbing than long, painful, sleepless nights. When they get ill, even for a brief time, it's the end of their world. They demand healing.

When you have been ill for most of your life, you understand that healing is grace. A cure is not always possible. And yet people pass hurtful comments and cause added misery because of their lack of compassion. They are not walking with Christ even if they believe they are. This is dangerous and to be prayed over.

I'll be fine. Because I have Paul who loves me despite my tantrums, the dramas and my impossible impatience. I have Rebecca, my daughter. My family. I may live in pain. I may even get fed up, but I have love and I have blessings. It's God's Will. I won't argue with that.

LETTING GO

Behind anger and bitterness lies fear. Who wants or dares to admit to being afraid? Not me. Or most people. To be scared is to be weak and vulnerable and we daren't claim these feelings for they overwhelm us. Angry people blame others for their problems. Failing to accept responsibility for personal choices. Failing to live with the consequences of their actions. I'm not an expert on such psychological issues, but I know what anger feels like. It's red and hot and extremely empowering. It makes you grit your teeth and snarl at the world. It creeps up on you and settles very nicely into the defence mechanism. It's easier to be angry than to be scared. To believe that everyone else is wrong and you're always right. Angry people don't have many friends. Because anger makes you self-absorbed, self-opinionated and self-righteous. Holding onto something so strong, so destructive, is easier than letting go. You can't let go until you know what you are letting go of. No-one wants to feel anger, but it's an easier option. It lets you off the proverbial hook. It's functional when it works if, indeed, it works at all. Angry souls deny vigorously, "Me? No, I'm fine. It's you that's got the problem".

Anger is self-perpetuating. It's passed on in families and turns children into murderers. No-one wins. Anger helps you to believe that you've won but it's an illusion. It breeds a deep unhappiness that causes confusion. Both physically and emotionally. Angry people rarely see their blessings. They are too busy transferring their dissatisfaction onto others. The weakest will absorb its transference and the myth will continue. Us against the world, "We'll show them!" Angry people don't know who they are. So they search for the impossible and blame their fate on bad genes or bad luck. Because that's a damn sight easier than blaming yourself. There is no authenticity here and quick fixes fade because issues aren't examined.

I believe that my anger is, and was, reactive. A natural reaction to unnatural events. Only it started to eat me up. It held me together for a long time, but I never felt "real". I wasn't true to myself. Only pretending to be funny and kind. My heart was like a stone – this didn't feel comfortable, but it felt safe. I could not handle what lay beneath the anger. Fear, angst and a bitterness that was starting to settle. Counselling got me out of denial and enabled me to "let go" of a lot of the anger. Fear is tricky, for it is so painful and big that to face it is to die. Fear of separation and fear of living. Fear of dying. Fear is incapacitating. It's huge and ugly. But it won't go away until you challenge it. I was fortunate to have Randolph to help me work through these strong emotions. It's easier to drink a few pints or pop a pill, and I would not condemn that because I've tried that too. It doesn't work. It gives you a hangover and the problem, the fear, becomes even bigger.

Anger breeds anxiety. Panicky emotions of dread. Sweaty palms and a sense of unreality that convinces you that your madness is almost a trait. But anxiety is a part of everyday living. Few admit to these bouts of instability for fear of being judged. I would be extremely wary of a person who claims never to have experienced anxiety. It's what they suppress but cannot give a name to. It's what makes us real and warm and human. I am convinced of that.

To understand the nature of our fear. To give anxiety a face. To embrace our powerlessness is a huge leap of human understanding. It makes us equal. Regardless of title, successes and failures we all desire acceptance. We want someone to embrace our aloneness and make things right. We need one another and are ashamed of the neediness for it creates a vulnerability that chokes. A smallness that confuses and disturbs.

The bitter fact is that, although we think we have control over our lives, the truth is that circumstances can change in the blink of an eye. An accident, for instance. Natural disasters. We think we have got it taped and . . . bang! We are forced to confront the big issue and it is not a happy place. So we rationalise and pass logical comments. Try to reason when reason is absent. Go round in circles until it eventually creeps up and makes us ill.

I recently met a wonderful Anglican priest, Rev. Michael Bennett, in Lourdes. The place of faith and hope and love. Where pain is applauded and handed over to the Mother of God.

We were chatting at the airport lounge in Manchester. He saw right through my soul and was determined to help me. We exchanged stories and he asked me whether I ever prayed for the Holy Spirit. To fill me with God's love. My answer was "no". It was unnerving, especially in such a holy place. I had to admit to my lack of trust. I cringed and shuddered, but it's true.

Rev. Michael assured me that God loved me very much and He desired my healing. He spoke of God's love of all of us. There was a great uneasiness on my part to pray for myself. Catholic preoccupation with sin and unworthiness. Fear of not pleasing God by refusing this cross. The Rev. said that although I had a lot of love for other people, I found it difficult to love myself. To value God's gifts of compassion and healing.

The Catholic church as an establishment has not been too successful in teaching us about God's love. It has rigid rules and regulations which are sometimes necessary but which can be damaging to a hurting soul. Confession is a healing grace, not a list of evil wrongdoings. We are taught to accept without asking too many questions. God doesn't want the perfect side of us. He desires all of us. The fear and the worry and the anger. He wants our wretched humanity and He alone can make us whole.

A stranger told me at the hotel bar how he and his wife had prayed for me that afternoon. I was so deeply touched. They didn't even know my name, but they had loved a fellow pilgrim.

And love is what holds us together. Acts of love, both big and small. Compassion most of all. The Holy Spirit spoke to the couple who prayed for me. In my ignorance, I have always believed that you must intercede for others before yourself. Psychological punishment, penance. Mortification of the psyche, perhaps. I must work on this, be grateful for my blessings and leave the rest to the all-knowing, all-loving creator God. You and I are incapable of "letting go" of poor hurts on our own. Memories are too vivid, visions too clear. We are human beings with wounded hearts, but we are pilgrims journeying in the same love, the same purpose. We desire peace above all else. Only God can give us this grace. And so we must ask with a meek and humble heart. A person who possesses God's peace has treasure indeed. This is the peace I crave. God will grant it to me when He thinks I need it. Until then, I'll pray and hope and thank him for the ride.

OH LORD, HEAR MY PRAYER

What is prayer? A soliloquy? A dialogue? A cry for help, or just an ordinary conversation between friends?

My prayer life leaves a lot to be desired. I'm too stiff and uncomfortable to remain still. My sinfulness looms when I attempt to make contact with a living God. Maybe that's why, subconsciously, I prefer to ask the saints to intercede on my behalf. I cringe at my littleness before my Almighty. I swear too much, sin too much. But I make contact because I know that He is there. How do I know? Why should I know? Why should the God of all creation grace a working-class girl? Why should He come to someone who has argued and had tantrums and sulked more times than I care to remember? He knows that He has scared me. Hurt me. Confused me. Left me to rot in my illness, my shame. There's plenty more fish in the sea.

He bothers with me because He knows that I believe in Him. He knows that I am a weak and self-willed human being. He knows everything about me. He loves me. And You. Jesus knows about my cursing, my anger, my pompous self-righteousness. I know that He exists. I have no doubt at all.

I believe in a merciful God, who became human for a purpose. Not for the delight of hanging on a cross for the unbelievers to mock and jeer. He came to make things right with the Father and us. He came to offer love and forgiveness. To make death a thing of the past. To bring comfort to us in the here and now. To reunite us with loved ones who have died.

I believe in Heaven. Not because I kid myself about joyful reunions but because of a deep conviction. Why should I fill my heart with nonsense if it were not the truth? I haven't seen Josie for over fourteen years. I've missed her on earth. Nothing can be worse than this. I don't know when I'll see her or my parents again, but I will. I know I will. This is my faith. My gift.

Revealed to a sinner. Grace revealed to an unworthy warrior who loves writing about the Gospels. I could write without belief. But I wouldn't be very convincing.

I don't claim to have any special insight. I don't understand the reasons for suffering, so why should He waste his time on me? I don't know. He knocked on my door and I let Him in. Reluctantly maybe, but I said "yes".

Somewhere along the dark and lonely road we connected.

Prayer to me is a conversation. It does not have to be formal. Just a chat. A thank you. Then a long list of "pleases" . . . I pray every day. Mostly at night. In the daytime if someone has asked me and is in big trouble. I wish I could be more holy in my approach to prayer but I don't think its always necessary. One sincere prayer is worth a hundred parrot-fashion Hail Marys.

I might pray when I'm driving. If someone is ill and my nerves are shaky I pray for guidance. I pray for courage to face suffering individuals. Because I know that I cannot manage on my own strength. That's not false humility. It's the truth.

My illness makes me unable to cope with excessive stress. Long-term steroid use depresses the body's ability to handle stress. So I struggle and God does the rest.

When I really concentrate, I'll say a few Hail Marys and my breathing slows down. I feel a warm, tingly feeling. An experience of being heard and loved. And accepted. This is the closest spiritual thing that's happened to me. Closeness in prayer. So much more if I spent more time praying instead of watching Discovery Health on TV.

I recall when Anne was having complications after Rachel, her youngest, was born. Things were dire and she was taken to theatre. I asked Claire to pray. I washed up. Begged God, leaning against the kitchen sink, to help Anne and I promised Him the earth if he saved her. He did. I thanked Him and went back to my old ways of taking God's grace for granted. How dare I?

Distractions during prayer used to irritate me. Now I just carry on. I'll be asking God's help and remember that I haven't switched the TV plugs off. Niggly worries will come, and that's fine. God understands. It's just like talking to a friend. Our minds wander, no matter how interested and faithful we are.

God is a friend. Not an enemy. And where reverence is necessary formality is OK. But it's not a must. God never stood on ceremony. Jesus never pretended. He was real. A perfect human being. He wasn't false. He didn't suffer fools gladly and He blessed sinners and saints. We don't have to get dolled up to pray.

All He desires is our hearts. It's so simple. It has been complicated by man-made rules and regulations. All He wants is for us to acknowledge Him as God, the Omnipotent One. He desires a love for His Blessed Mother and He wants us to keep His name. Jesus Christ.

I don't like terms like piety and religion. I much prefer

faith and spirituality. Faith in action. Charity and devotion of those like Mother Teresa of Calcutta. Self-emptying and humble. Such a small, holy body had statesmen and dignitaries in awe. They knew she possessed something divine, a love of God, so beautiful that it founded a religious order – Missionaries of Charity – against all odds. It started with a "call within a call". God told her to go out and feed the hungry. Respect the dying and the dirty. The maggot-filled wounds. She answered His call. Never once did she claim glory or money for herself, it was all for the poorest of the poor.

They said that she should concentrate on changing the political face of the slums. She left that to others. Her job was to drag orphans from dustbins and cradle the dying.

Saint Padre Pio and Mother Teresa led prayerful lives. Hours dedicated to the veneration of the Blessed Sacrament. They prayed for you and I. We can't all be like the dear old Friar and Mother Teresa. Such people are sent by God as torches in a darkened world. The little nun saw greater poverty in the western world. A poverty of spirit which disturbed her more than anything. Lack of charity for one another, shattered lives that could not be assuaged by goods. We need that love she showed, in the ghettos of Calcutta. We need that oneness with God.

The world recognised Padre Pio and Mother Teresa during their lifetime. They took the flack like other saints but they showed us how it's done. Through sacrifice, love, charity and prayer. God took care of the rest.

And so it is with us. When the nights are long and lonely, when your heart is breaking and there seems no way out, we must pray. To ask Our Lord for courage and strength. Tell Him our troubles and strife. He's heard it all before. He will listen as if He is hearing it for the first time. Because life is a prayer. Breath is a blessing. A caress is a sacred embrace. Sweeter still, because of the troubles. Because of the pressures and the hardships we must all face. We cannot avoid the "dark night of the soul". One thing's for sure, we cannot stand it on our own. That's why God sent His Son. That is why He shed His precious blood. So that in our human misery, in spite of our unworthiness and because of it, when we pray and when we ask, He will come to our aid. He will comfort us. Sustain us. He will hold out His arms and shield us under His heavy cloak. Because He is Our Father and that's what dads do.

PRAYER
TO SAINT PHILOMENA

O God, who didst wonderfully strengthen
Thy Blessed Virgin and Martyr
Philomena in her sufferings and
didst glorify her, by so many miracles,
grant us, through her intercession,
that in the adversities of this life,
we may always participate in
Thy Grace and protection.
Amen.

Further information about Saint Philomena can be obtained from:
The Association of Saint Philomena's Friends
P.O. Box 13
HOLYWELL
CH8 7WW
Wales